USA TODAY

Lifeline

BIOGRAPHIES

SERGEY BRIN AND LARRY PAGE

Founders of Google

by Stephanie Sammartino McPherson

T F C B

Twenty-First Century Books · Minneapolis

For my husband, Richard, and daughters, Jennifer and Marianne, with love and thanks

Twenty-First Century Books
A division of Lerner Publishing Group, Inc.
241 First Avenue North
Minneapolis, MN 55401 U.S.A.

Website address: www.lernerbooks.com

Library of Congress Cataloging-in-Publication Data

McPherson, Stephanie Sammartino.
    Sergey Brin and Larry Page : founders of Google / by Stephanie Sammartino McPherson.
        p.   cm. — (USA Today Lifeline biographies)
    Includes bibliographical references and index.
    ISBN 978-0-7613-5221-1 (lib. bdg. : alk. paper)
    1. Brin, Sergey, 1973– 2. Page, Larry, 1973– 3. Computer programmers—United States—Biography. 4. Businesspeople—United States—Biography. 5. Internet programming—United States. 6. Google (Firm) 7. Google. 8. Web search engines.
I. Title.
QA76.2.A2M37 2011
005.1092'2—dc22 [B]   2010001034

Manufactured in the United States of America
1 – VI – 7/15/10

USA TODAY | **Lifeline** BIOGRAPHIES

NASDAQ®

Public offering: Larry Page *(center)* takes part in the ceremony that officially listed Google on the NASDAQ stock exchange in August 2004. He is surrounded by Google executives and NASDAQ representatives.

Instant Billionaires

The ritual is a familiar one on Wall Street in the financial district of New York City. At the beginning of each business day, an official rings the bell, signifying the opening of the NASDAQ stock exchange. The routine never varies.

But on August 19, 2004, an unusual excitement buzzed through the room. A smiling but nervous young man stood facing the crowd of stockbrokers and businesspeople. The honor of ringing the bell fell to this newcomer, Larry Page. Less than six years earlier, he had cofounded Google with his friend Sergey Brin. Immediately, the company had mushroomed into an astounding phenomenon, confounding financial experts. On this day, for the first time ever, Google was selling shares of its company to the public. The financial term for such an occasion is an *initial public offering*, or IPO. Google's going public generated so much excitement that *Newsweek* magazine called it "the century's most anticipated IPO."

In its brief history, the Google search engine had stunned people in all walks of life. From pop culture to space exploration, from history to bargain shopping, people could use Google to find almost anything they wanted to know. Everyone appreciated the way it cut through the jungle of information on the Internet at lightning speed. Within one year of its founding in 1998, Google was handling 3 million search requests a day. Two years later, in 2001, Google processed 100 million search queries each day. Would Google's popularity spell financial

Cofounders: Sergey Brin *(left)* and Larry Page *(right)* started Google in 1998. The two met while they were graduate students at Stanford University in California.

success in the stock market? Would people who bought Google stock make money on their investments? Businesspeople, scientists, educators, and ordinary computer users were eager to see what would happen with Google stock.

Larry may have felt awkward, dressed in suit and tie, in the formal surroundings of the NASDAQ Exchange. The environment could not have been more different from the freedom and relaxed atmosphere of the Googleplex, the company's headquarters in Mountain View, California. Larry and Sergey are casual guys. They had carefully cultivated a comfortable, creative, and fun workspace. The Googleplex boasted volleyball courts, a billiard table, a piano, and a gourmet cafeteria. Employees were even allowed to bring their dogs to work. While Larry rang the bell in New York, Sergey, probably dressed in Levi's, an old T-shirt, and Crocs or in-line skates, kept things running in Mountain View.

"This is not a traditional company," Larry and Sergey had written before Google went public. They were referring to much more than the unconventional setting. Almost everything about Google was unexpected—even the way it began. As graduate students at Stanford University, Larry and Sergey didn't set out to create a search engine. But as they pursued their computer research, they realized they had the makings of a search engine more efficient than any that existed. They didn't plan to start a company so early in their careers. But as more people began using Google, the inexperienced young men took the plunge into business. They didn't anticipate going public with their company. But they managed to do so without giving up their control of Google. Finally, they never sought to become wealthy. But when the NASDAQ closed the day of their IPO, Larry and Sergey, both only thirty-one years of age, had become billionaires.

And the story of Google was just beginning.

www.usatoday.com

USA TODAY

Money

SECTION B

May 5, 2004

First there was Beatlemania, now there's Googlemania

From the Pages of
USA TODAY

If there were still an *Ed Sullivan Show*, the Google founders would get a guest slot, maybe right after [singer] Robert Goulet.

Google is as big as the Beatles. Founders Sergey Brin and Larry Page are getting the white-hot celebrity treatment. They've been all over the news and on magazine covers. Next they'll probably be guest cartoons on *The Simpsons*, wear frothy white moustaches in a Got Milk? ad, and sit by Paula Abdul as visiting critics on *American Idol*.

But ever since last week's announcement of an initial public offering, the Google frenzy has been off the charts. And it's going to get more clamorous because—intentionally or not—Brin and Page are pitch-perfect in the way they're playing on public sentiment during the IPO process.

Of course, Google is a phenomenon with or without an IPO. From U.S. users alone, Google processes 1 billion searches a month. The Beatles have sold 1 billion LPs and 45s worldwide in their history. Even if a better comparison is the number of times a Beatles song is played, it's unlikely that ever surpassed 1 billion a month in the USA.

Strictly by the statistics, Google probably touches more lives than the Beatles did in the late 1960s.

It's not just the numbers. Google has infiltrated the daily lives of millions of people. It is beloved. It's not merely a Web site, but a trusted friend, a helper—a rather unintelligent thing that we humans anthropomorphize, choosing to believe it is something more. It's the Lassie of the Web.

It will, Page insists, operate under the banner, "Don't be evil"—as if there is a surfeit of companies out there that go by the slogan, "Be evil."

Maybe it's not so different from those other chaps who said, "All you need is love."

—Kevin Maney

Computers in the 1970s: Large mainframe computers like these were used in the 1970s. Larry Page's family was lucky enough to have a home computer by the late 1970s.

Larry Page: Big Dreams

Even as a little boy, Larry Page found computers fascinating. He was born in Lansing, Michigan, on March 26, 1973. At that time, personal computers were still in the early stages of development. Although government offices and universities had enormous mainframe computers, individuals rarely had their own home computers.

Larry's household was different. "We were lucky enough to get our first home computer in 1978," Larry has recalled. "It was huge, and it cost a lot of money, and we couldn't afford to eat well after that."

But the Pages thought the financial sacrifice was worth it. Larry's parents, Carl Victor and Gloria, taught computer science at Michigan State University. They had met when they were both computer students at the University of Michigan in Ann Arbor. Their first son, Carl Jr., caught the "computer bug" early on. In turn, Carl Jr. shared his interest in computers and electronic devices with Larry, nine years his junior.

Strong Grandfathers

Larry's grandfather Page was proud of his family's achievements. He had spent his life working on an automobile assembly line. Ambitious for the future, he was determined to give his children the education he had never had. Larry knew the story of how his grandpa had taken his young children, Carl and Beverly, to see the University of Michigan. "That is where you're going to go to college," he declared.

Both Larry's grandfathers left him a legacy of courage and commitment to social justice. His father's father took part in an important autoworkers' strike in 1937 in Flint, Michigan. The bold stance he took with his fellow employees helped force General Motors to recognize the United Auto Workers as the employee's union. Larry's mother's father also showed strength of character when he moved to Israel. He settled in Arad, near the Dead Sea, where he endured an extremely harsh desert environment. Working as a tool and die maker, he did his part to make the struggling community successful.

Larry had a happy childhood. Although his parents divorced when he was eight years old, he felt very close to both his father and mother. He looked forward to the Grateful Dead rock concerts he sometimes attended with his father. He also got to know and appreciate his father's second wife. "A professor's life is pretty flexible," Larry once said. "He was able to spend oodles of time raising me. Could there be a better upbringing than university brat?"

"Interested in Stuff"

As a youngster, Larry attended a Montessori school. The school allowed him to explore his own interests and learn at his own pace. At home he had all the enrichment a scientifically inclined boy could want. As new computers became available through the years, the Pages added them to their collection. Larry became the first child in his elementary school to hand in a paper written on a word processer. The teachers were astonished. "They didn't know what a dot matrix printer was," Larry recalled. Undoubtedly, the gifted young student was happy to explain it to them.

Larry missed little when it came to the latest developments in technology. He enjoyed reading copies of the magazine *Popular Science*, as well as other journals that lay around his house. "I just got interested in stuff," he explained, "technology and how devices work." Carl Jr. encouraged his curiosity. Larry was only nine years old when his brother started college at the University of Michigan. Often he shared his computer homework with Larry.

Carl Jr. also showed Larry how to dismantle common household items to see how they worked. Eagerly, Larry tackled almost anything he could get his hands on, including a set of his father's power tools. According to one version of the story, Larry couldn't put the tools back together again. But Larry laughingly denies that account. He claims that he could have reassembled the tools. "I just didn't," he says.

Larry was even more interested in building devices than in taking them apart. "From a very early age, I . . . realized I wanted to invent things." All sorts of ideas churned in his resourceful mind.

Nikola Tesla

When he was twelve years old, Larry came across a biography of an eccentric inventor named Nikola Tesla. The genius of the Croatian-born Tesla fascinated Larry. Tesla's experiments with electricity and physics had led to such modern marvels as laser beams, remote controls, fluorescent lights, and radio. He also designed a system for distributing electricity to homes and businesses that is still in use.

Maria Montessori

Born in 1870 in Ancona, Italy, Maria Montessori became the first woman to graduate from medical school at the University of Rome. As a young doctor, or *dottoressa*, she became interested in helping children with emotional and mental problems. She believed that if these children were placed in a sensory-rich environment, their natural curiosity would lead them to explore their world and to learn.

Soon Maria realized that what would work for children with mental problems would work for all children. On January 6, 1906, she opened her first school, called the Casa dei Bambini (House of Children) in Rome, Italy. Two years later, she published her book, *The Montessori Method*, and began training teachers in her special techniques. Maria got such good results with children that her ideas rapidly spread. By 1911 the United States had its first Montessori school in Tarrytown, New York.

Larry and Sergey remember their Montessori years fondly. In 2004 they were listed among "The 10 Most Fascinating People of 2004" in a Barbara Walters ABC-TV Special. Walters mentioned that both young men were the children of college professors. She wondered if this had something to do with their

New school: Italian doctor and teacher Maria Montessori founded a school in the early 1900s using special techniques to teach and engage children. Larry Page and Sergey Brin attended Montessori schools in their childhoods.

success. No, they replied. Instead, they thanked their Montessori education for instilling confidence and encouraging creativity in them.

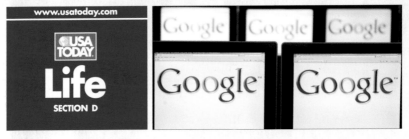
Taking Tesla as a role model, Larry dreamed of making important technological advances.

But as exciting as this would be, Larry knew that he had to do more. Tesla had been a poor businessman who allowed others to implement his ideas for him. He died in poverty. Larry wanted to control the future of his own creations. That would mean establishing a business to promote his products. It was an exhilarating prospect for an aspiring inventor. "Probably from when I was 12, I knew I was going to start a company eventually," Larry recalls.

Larry loved to read. Whatever his family packed for vacations in Oregon, they always made sure to leave one suitcase empty. When the Pages returned home, the suitcase would be full of books they bought at the famous Powell's bookstore in Portland, Oregon.

"Always Ahead"

Larry's childhood wasn't all computers and electronics. He enjoyed Boy Scouts in middle school. He liked music and played the saxophone in his high school band. Larry was so good that he was chosen to attend a highly selective summer music camp in Interlochen, Michigan.

Successful in school: Larry, shown here in a high school yearbook photo, excelled at his studies in high school and college. He majored in engineering at the University of Michigan.

According to his brother, Larry's interests ranged beyond science and music to "social things, government, politics, everything." Larry always welcomed a good debate about issues or ideas. In this regard, he took after his father. Carl enjoyed explaining his own views and challenging the opinions of those with whom he disagreed—even his sons. Larry sharpened his wits in these good-natured exchanges.

Larry's father had strong ideas about where his son should attend college. "We'll pay for any school you want to go to," he joked, "as long as it's Michigan." In 1991, at the age of eighteen, Larry followed in his parents' and his brother's footsteps by entering the University of Michigan. His academic performance soon earned him a reputation as an outstanding student. "Larry just stood out," recalled one of his professors. "He was always ahead." Larry's classmates agreed. They elected him president of the university's chapter of Eta Kappa Nu, an honor society for computer students. Although quiet, Larry was friendly. He was just as comfortable staffing the organization's doughnut stand on campus as he was leading the meetings.

LeaderShape was another university program that claimed Larry's attention. Aiming to develop future leaders, the directors urged participants to have a "healthy disregard for the impossible." Larry took the motto to heart. He wanted to change the transportation system on campus. It certainly seemed impossible, but that didn't stop Larry from seeking an energy-efficient alternative to the buses that ran through campus. He thought a monorail would be a cleaner, better way for students to get around. Although Larry couldn't persuade

IN FOCUS

Creating with Legos

In college Larry used Lego blocks to build an inkjet printer. "I built all the electronics and mechanics to drive it," he explains. "I like to be able to do those kinds of things." Larry used his big Lego printer to print giant posters. Legos still hold a special place in Larry's heart. In the early days of Google, he and Sergey Brin made Lego cabinets to hold computers. When a reporter asked him his favorite technology, Larry replied, "The thing I'm most fond of is Lego Mindstorms [Lego kits with computers]. I've been doing some classified things with them."

university officials to build a monorail, he did join a school team to design a solar car. Instead of gasoline, the car Larry helped develop ran on power from the sun. Named the Maize & Blue after the school colors, the solar car competed in two races and took eleventh place in the 1993 World Solar Challenge for solar cars.

In 1995 Larry received his degree in engineering with honors that included the school's first Outstanding Student Award. Solar-powered vehicles continued to intrigue him. "You never lose a dream," he told graduates of his alma mater in 2009. "It just incubates as a hobby." But Larry knew his immediate future lay in computers—not in transportation. Like his father, he wanted to earn a doctoral degree. To his delight, Stanford University in Palo Alto, California, accepted him into its PhD program. Stanford was known for its excellent computer department. In addition, it was located near Silicon Valley, an area near San Francisco where thousands of computer and electronic companies had headquarters. "I always wanted to go to Silicon Valley," Larry recalled later.

Despite his excitement, Larry was cautious. He wanted to make certain that Stanford was really right for him. In the spring of 1995, before he accepted Stanford's offer, Larry flew to California for a tour of the university and of nearby San Francisco. He liked the sprawling campus, the exciting city, and the excellent computer department. But Larry thought the student guide who took him through San Francisco was "pretty obnoxious." The other people in the group must have been startled. Larry and the guide argued about almost everything. The guide was an energetic, supremely confident computer student named Sergey Brin.

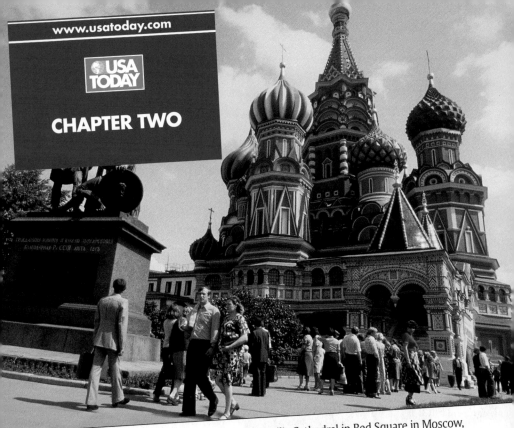

Russian childhood: People stroll near Saint Basil's Cathedral in Red Square in Moscow, Russia, in 1980. Sergey Brin was born in Moscow and lived there until he was almost six.

Sergey Brin: Grateful American

Sergey Brin spent his earliest years half a world away from the midwestern United States where Larry grew up. Sergey was born on August 21, 1973, in Moscow in what was then the Soviet Union (modern-day Russia and fourteen other republics). Compared to many Soviets, Sergey's family was fairly well off. Both his parents had college degrees and good jobs. Michael Brin worked as an economist for the government's central planning agency called GOSPLAN. Eugenia Brin had a job in the research lab of an important industrial school, the Soviet Oil and Gas Institute. The family, which included Sergey's paternal grandmother, lived in a small apartment in the middle of Moscow. Despite the crowded conditions, the Brins were lucky to have their own place. Many families in Moscow were forced to share apartments.

Eugenia was fairly happy with her situation. Although Michael was generally content too, he had some serious grievances. Michael had wanted to become an astronomer. But that career was denied him because he was Jewish. The Communist Party, which controlled the Soviet Union, discriminated against Jews. Soviet Jews were not allowed to enter universities or study physics. Michael had been able to get around some rules (even earning a PhD), but the government refused to let him study astronomy.

In 1977 Michael traveled to Warsaw, Poland, to attend an international mathematics conference. After enjoying open, uncensored discussions with colleagues from all over Europe and the United States, Michael understood freedom in a new way. "We cannot stay here any more," he declared on arriving back in Moscow. He wanted to emigrate to the United States.

At four years old, Sergey could not understand much of the discussions that followed between his parents. But perhaps he sensed that their talks had something to do with him. Although Eugenia didn't want to leave Moscow, she finally realized that Sergey would have a better future in the United States. He would be able to do whatever he wished without facing the intolerance that had thwarted Michael and her.

Journey to a New Life
In September 1978, the Brins filed an application to leave the Soviet Union. GOSPLAN immediately fired Michael. Under pressure, Eugenia quit her job too. Each found other work to tide them over while they

waited for their paperwork to be processed. By then five years old, Sergey was ready for preschool. But his parents didn't think much of the local school he would attend. They kept Sergey home and took turns watching him. His only playground was the barren courtyard of his family's apartment building.

In May 1979, the paperwork was approved. The Brins were fortunate to receive their visas so quickly. Some Soviet Jews never received permission to emigrate. In fact, not long afterward, the government put an end to all Jewish emigration.

Meanwhile, Sergey found himself leaving the only home and neighborhood he had ever known. The lengthy trip must have been confusing to a little boy, almost six. First, the family went to Vienna, Austria, and then on to Paris, France, where Michael took a brief job. On October 25, the family landed at Kennedy Airport in New York. Sergey stared in amazement at the traffic as friends from Moscow drove the Brins to Long Island. He had never seen so many huge cars.

Finally, the Brins settled in Maryland, where Michael took a job teaching math at the University of Maryland. Their cinder block home, though small, was nicer than the cramped apartment in Moscow. And the nearby Montessori school provided resources and enrichment that Sergey could not have experienced in a Russian preschool. Soon he was happily exploring his new educational environment. He especially liked multiplication games, puzzles, and maps. Fitting in with his classmates was another matter, however. He was shy with the other children. They could not understand what he said because of his thick accent.

Gifted Student

By the time he was nine years old, Sergey sounded more like an American. That was the year his parents gave him his first computer, a Commodore 64. The delighted youngster began exploring the Internet and playing computer games. He even created his own computer game, complete with virtual warriors. Not surprisingly, a boy who enjoyed computers also liked math. Sometimes Sergey sat around listening

Visiting the Homeland

Just before Sergey turned seventeen, his father took some high school math students on an exchange program to the Soviet Union. His family accompanied him. Believing that the government wielded too much power over Soviet citizens, Sergey felt uneasy and angry. He gave vent to his emotions by throwing some small rocks at a police car. The officers inside were not amused. Sergey may have felt a pang of regret when they emerged from the car frowning. Luckily Sergey's parents were able to pass the incident off as a childish prank. But Sergey felt truly uncomfortable in the repressive Soviet regime. Only two days into the trip, he told his father, "Thank you for taking us all out of Russia."

while his father discussed mathematics with colleagues. He was still very young when he ventured a solution to a challenging math problem. At first Michael Brin paid little attention. After all, his students at the University of Maryland had not been able to solve the problem. How could Sergey? It took a family friend and mathematician to point out to Michael that his son's solution was correct!

Sergey's education extended beyond math and science. He attended a Hebrew school for almost three years. Jewish families often send their children to Hebrew school to learn Hebrew, the traditional language of Jews. The Brins were not particularly religious, but they appreciated all that the Jewish community had done for them when they first arrived in Maryland. And they honored their heritage by celebrating Passover, an important Jewish holiday. Sergey took an interest in Jewish culture, especially after he visited Israel, a Jewish state in the Middle East, at the age of eleven. He never made his bar mitzvah, however, partly because he felt uncomfortable receiving the gifts and money that often accompany that rite of passage for Jewish boys when they turn thirteen.

As he grew up, Sergey enjoyed reading books by Richard Feynman. A leading physicist, Feynman had helped develop the atomic bomb during World War II (1939–1945). Many years later, he helped investigate the tragedy of the space shuttle *Challenger*. Feynman was also a musician and a storyteller with a great sense of humor. He published both technical books and popular autobiographical books such as the best-selling *Surely You're Joking, Mr. Feynman.* "It seemed like a very great life he lived," Sergey later recalled. "Aside from making really big contributions in his own field, he was pretty broad-minded. I remember he had an excerpt where he was explaining how he really wanted to be a Leonardo [da Vinci], an artist and a scientist. I found that pretty inspiring."

In 1987 Sergey's brother Sam was born. Suddenly Sergey wasn't an only child anymore. In fact, at the age of thirteen, Sergey probably didn't feel much like a child at all. He breezed through middle school, astounding teachers with his mathematical skills. Math came so easily to Sergey that he sometimes tried to teach the teachers. He thought nothing of pitting his techniques and answers against theirs. When he was fifteen, Sergey began taking math classes at the University of Maryland. Few people were surprised when he graduated high school in three years instead of the usual four.

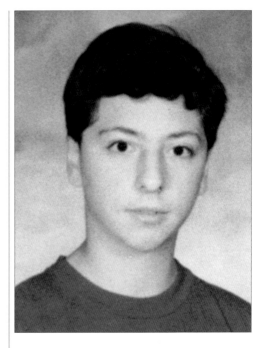

Gifted student: Sergey excelled in school, especially in math classes. He started taking college classes when he was still in high school.

IN FOCUS

Helping Others

In 2009, thirty years after Sergey's arrival in the United States, he donated one million dollars to the Hebrew Immigrant Aid Society, the same group that had helped the Brins relocate. "I would have never had the kinds of opportunities I've had here in the Soviet Union, or even in Russia today," Sergey told the *New York Times*. "I would like to see any one be able to achieve their dreams, and that's what this organization does."

The University of Maryland didn't prove to be much of a challenge either. Again, Sergey graduated in three years. A National Science Foundation scholarship enabled him to apply to some of the top graduate schools in the country. Determined to get a doctoral degree in computer science, Sergey decided to attend Stanford. It would give him a chance to know a different and very beautiful part of the United States. And like Larry Page, he was greatly attracted by the nearness of Silicon Valley.

Stanford suited Sergey just fine. He enjoyed the people, loved the climate, and took readily to popular sports such as in-line skating and skiing. Energetic, slight but strong, he also excelled at gymnastics and took trapeze lessons. Academics seemed to take a backseat to athletics. Once his father asked him whether he had chosen any advanced classes. Not skipping a beat, Sergey replied, "Yes, advanced swimming." Sergey's relaxed manners and friendliness made him a perfect selection for leading tours of prospective students around San Francisco. Then he found someone who disagreed with almost everything he said. Sergey had been at Stanford for almost two years when he met Larry Page.

CHAPTER THREE

Stanford students: Larry and Sergey attended Stanford University in California. Stanford is in the San Francisco area, shown here beyond the Golden Gate Bridge.

Larry and Sergey

San Francisco is a city of steep hillsides, clattering cable cars, and the sweeping arc of the Golden Gate Bridge. It's hard to imagine quarreling when so many interesting things compete for one's attention. But on the tour of the city for prospective Stanford students, Sergey and Larry argued vigorously. Whatever one said, the other seemed to take immediate issue with. Yet although they considered each other "obnoxious," they couldn't really dislike each other. Each enjoyed a spirited discussion, and they shared a fierce academic competitiveness and passion for computers. When Larry returned to Stanford as a student that fall, he ran into Sergey again. The two resumed their bantering in a friendly sort of way.

During Larry's second semester, a new computer center, named after Microsoft founder Bill Gates, opened at Stanford. Although they were assigned to different offices, Sergey was soon spending most of his time in Larry's room at the computer center. Four other graduate students also shared the crowded space. They fixed it up as a home away from home with hanging plants, a sleeping pad, and even a piano plugged into a computer. Almost any hour of the day or night, students could be found in room 360.

"They were fun guys to share an office with," Tamara Munser, an office mate, recalled of Larry and Sergey, or LarryandSergey, as people often slurred their names together. But they talked so much that sometimes she had to block out their chatter with headphones to get any work done. No topic was too serious or silly for them to tackle. Could they make a structure as big as a building out of lima beans? they debated one day. The dispute got quite loud. It didn't matter that

Computer center: Sergey and Larry had offices at the new Bill Gates computer center on the Stanford campus.

Larry and Sergey had no intention of building anything out of lima beans. They had fun clashing about it.

During this busy period, Larry's father contracted pneumonia. Carl Page had had polio as a child, and his lungs had been damaged. Unable to withstand the severity of the infection, he died. Larry was overcome with grief. But he had good friends, including Sergey, to comfort him. And his older brother lived nearby in Silicon Valley. Together, they dealt with the devastating loss.

Larry knew how much his education had meant to his father. Both he and Sergey were still looking for dissertation topics. To receive a PhD, a candidate has to complete an original research project and a scholarly paper. Larry and Sergey would have to spend a long time developing and writing their papers. The subjects needed to be relevant, challenging, and interesting to hold their attention over a long period. Larry had narrowed his search to three possible topics. His dissertation professor, Dr. Terry Winograd, strongly favored one of them. "Why don't you work on the Web for a while?" he suggested.

IN FOCUS

The Web and the Internet

The World Wide Web, or Web, is a vast body of interconnected documents, images, and videos that are accessible through the Internet. Although people sometimes confuse the Web with the Internet, the two are not the same. The Internet is a series of computer networks, sometimes called a "network of networks" that allow computers to communicate with one another. It existed before the World Wide Web. Without the Internet, there could be no sharing of information and Web pages between computers. The Web depends on the Internet for its existence just as Google depends on the Web for its existence.

Life

SECTION D

August 3, 1994

World Wide Web helps untangle Internet's labyrinth

<u>From the Pages of</u>
<u>USA TODAY</u>

For most people, the Internet is like an exotic South Seas island—an enticing destination, but too hard to reach.

But a new way to travel the Internet, the World Wide Web, may be just the ticket for people too intimidated to set foot on the information highway. It's the latest rage among Net aficionados. And technological barriers that have kept it out of the home are expected to fall within the next year or two.

The Web, used in tandem with a popular software "browsing" program called Mosaic, offers an easy, point-and-click way to cruise the worldwide computer network known as the Internet. There are no arcane commands to master. Information is presented a "page" at a time with photos, graphics—even sound clips and video.

But most home users reach the Internet indirectly through an on-line service, electronic bulletin board or local Internet provider. At the moment, most Web wanderers are college graduate students and corporate users who have access to high-end equipment.

But modems, the devices that link computers to phone lines, present a barrier. Currently, the fastest widely available home modems transfer 14,400 bits of information per second—too slow for satisfying Web cruising. Many experts feel 56,000 bits per second is the minimum acceptable rate.

Advances in technology are toppling those barriers. Most promising: the ability to link your computer to the Internet via the same cables that bring MTV and HBO to your home. Those lines can transfer data at 10 million bits per second. Several cable companies are experimenting with cable-Internet links. Also, phone companies are starting to offer direct Internet access.

These advances are driven by a certain urgency. Internet providers know the Net will not become a mass-market service until it's cheap and easy to use.

"It's got to be more like a car—step on the gas pedal and go," says Dataquest's Lisa Thorell. "You shouldn't need to be an Internet guru."

—David Landis

Where Did the World Wide Web Come From?

The story of the World Wide Web begins in the 1980s in Geneva, Switzerland. British computer programmer Tim Berners-Lee, working at a huge physics research lab called CERN, did not like the way the facility's computers stored information. Berners-Lee was in charge of keeping track of the many scientists' experiments and computer needs at CERN. The information was continually changing as new people came from all over the world and other scientists returned home. He became frustrated with the length of time it took him to access the information he needed. Because of the way material was stored, it often required many steps to retrieve a piece of information. Berners-Lee thought of a new way to store CERN's vast amount of data in a manner that required fewer steps for a person to find what he needed.

Berners-Lee started with a single page, which he called a node. The second page linked to the first. Every page in his system had to link to other pages through random associations. He named this innovative computer program Enquire, after a nineteenth-century encyclopedia he had browsed as a child. The Internet was still in its early stages when Berners-Lee created the first Enquire program. Most computers could not "talk," or communicate, easily with one another. But he knew this would change one day. "Suppose all the information stored on computers everywhere were linked," he suggested. "Suppose I could program my computer to create a space in which anything could be linked to anything."

Eventually that is exactly what he did. The documents in his new program were connected through hypertext links. That meant that certain highlighted words or phrases (hypertext) in a document would lead to other documents with more information. In Berners-Lee's computer program, every document was linked to one or more other documents. By then the Internet had begun to connect computers across the globe. Tim named his program the World Wide Web. It was up and running by Christmas Day 1990. Once computer users discovered the Web and began adding websites, its growth was unbounded.

That sounded fine to Larry. The World Wide Web fascinated him. Barely five years old, it was growing by leaps and bounds as more people created websites. Whatever a person wanted to know, there was certain to be something about it on the Web.

A Very Big Dream

Larry was so excited about his work on the World Wide Web that he even dreamed about it. One night he woke up with a sudden insight. "What if we could download the whole Web?" he wondered, "and just keep the links and . . . ." Larry's imagination rushed forward toward exciting possibilities. But he knew that dreams often vanish when morning comes. Snatching a pencil, he spent much of the night writing.

Larry told Sergey all about his idea to download the Web. Intrigued, Sergey thought about his work in "data mining." Something like mining Earth for precious stones, data mining consists of going through large numbers of facts, figures, and other materials in search of meaningful patterns and relationships. Although Sergey found the work fascinating, he still hadn't chosen his dissertation topic. Larry's plan held interesting possibilities. What could be more exciting than analyzing, or "mining," the huge amount of data on the World Wide Web? "I talked to lots of research groups," Sergey later recalled, "and this was the most interesting project, both because it tackled the Web, which represents human knowledge, and because I liked Larry and the other two people who were working with us." Larry and Sergey decided to collaborate. Whatever insights resulted from downloading the Web, they would discover them together.

 Larry shared the story of his fascinating dream at a commencement speech that he gave at his alma mater, the University of Michigan, in May 2009. "When a really great dream shows up, grab it!" he urged the new graduates.

CHAPTER FOUR

The Web: Even though the World Wide Web only had about ten million documents on it in 1996, it was still a daunting task to Larry and Sergey to download them all for their project.

BackRub to Google

Downloading the Web must have seemed like the computer equivalent of climbing Mount Everest. The Web numbered about ten million documents in 1996, and it was growing every day. In fact, in the course of each year, it grew more than 2,000 percent! But Larry still had a "healthy disregard for the impossible." He told his adviser, Dr. Winograd, that he expected the task to take several weeks. Although Winograd knew it would take much longer, he didn't tell Larry. He trusted Larry's instincts and didn't want to discourage him. Maybe something significant would come from downloading the Web. A faculty friend of Sergey's, a young professor from India, Rajeev Motwani, also found the project intriguing.

To begin their project, Larry and Sergey had to send out a crawler. Sometimes called a spider, or a robot, a crawler is a special program that visits websites and copies them. These copies are then used to create an index of the Web. The crawler also identifies links between websites. Using the crawler, Larry and Sergey would be able to see which links led into a website as well as what links led out of it. Exploring those links was crucial to their project.

Links are the heart of the World Wide Web, the glue that holds everything together. But Larry thought he detected a flaw in the Web's structure. You can easily see which links lead forward from (out of) a website. But what about the links that led into a website from other Web documents? These are called backlinks. Visitors to the site had no way of knowing how many links led into the site or where they came from. Larry and Sergey thought this was vital information.

In March 1996, Larry positioned the crawler to his own website: page@cs.stanford.edu. Before he could even turn around, the crawler had copied the contents and proceeded on its way. The downloading of the Web had officially begun. Larry dubbed the project BackRub since he was especially interested in studying backlinks on the Web.

Larry and Sergey reasoned that if a website had many links leading into it, it was a popular site. People had established the backlinks because they thought the site had good material. Some experts have

 As Larry set out to download the Web, he estimated that there were about 100 million links between websites. As the project took off, he realized that the number was far greater.

compared every link that leads into a website to a vote for that site. If a site has many votes, many people have found it useful.

But Larry and Sergey knew that not all backlinks were equal. Some were more important than others. Take the website of the popular marine park Sea World. If Sea World has a backlink from the University of California's Department of Marine Biology, that is more important than a backlink from a teenager's "I Love Dolphins" site. Larry and Sergey wanted a mathematical way to show which backlinks were more important than others. They could do this by counting the number of backlinks into these backlinks. The math became quite demanding.

Refusing to be daunted, Larry and Sergey developed a complicated equation called an algorithm. Using it, they were able to analyze not only the number of backlinks a website had but also the number of links into each of those backlinks. They called their elaborate system PageRank in honor of Larry Page, who had started the whole project rolling.

Larry and Sergey loved what they were doing. They didn't know what would come of their work, but they hoped to find something useful, something that might make a difference in the way people

IN FOCUS

A Difference in Style

Sergey's professor friend Rajeev Motwani remembered Larry and Sergey as "some of the smartest people I have ever met. But they were brilliant in different ways." He characterized Sergey as "a problem solver" and a "lightning fast" mathematician. Larry liked to mull things over more.

Motwani discussed individual visits they made to his office as a key to their personalities. Crackling with enthusiasm, Sergey would burst into the room without bothering to knock. Equally passionate about his work, Larry would nevertheless take the time to rap politely on the door.

used computers. "My goals were to work on something that would be academically real and interesting," Larry explained later. "But there is no reason if you are doing academic work to work on things that are impractical. I wanted both."

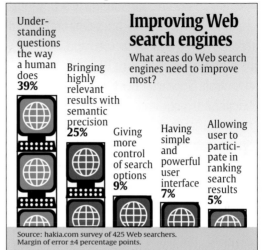

USA TODAY Snapshots®

Improving Web search engines

What areas do Web search engines need to improve most?

Understanding questions the way a human does
39%

Bringing highly relevant results with semantic precision
25%

Giving more control of search options
9%

Having simple and powerful user interface
7%

Allowing user to participate in ranking search results
5%

Source: hakia.com survey of 425 Web searchers.
Margin of error ±4 percentage points.

By Jae Yang and Bob Laird, USA TODAY, 2007

Gradually Larry and Sergey realized that they already had both—intellectual challenge and a useful application. In putting together their BackRub project, they had stumbled upon a method to improve Internet searches. If you entered a URL, or Web address, into BackRub, it listed the backlinks to the website in order of importance according to PageRank. If you considered the website as a topic to be investigated and the rated backlinks as responses, the whole process seemed to mimic a search engine, a program to help someone find information on the Web. But Larry and Sergey believed there was a difference. They believed that BackRub put the most relevant replies to the front. Existing search engines such as AltaVista and Excite did not do this. Instead, they cluttered their lists with all sorts of trivial results. "Why are they returning these results that are obviously not important?" Larry wondered.

Larry and Sergey concluded that backlinks held the key to really relevant search results. Their next step was only logical. Using PageRank, they restructured BackRub as a search engine. When they fed terms into the new BackRub, it gave much better results than any previous search engine. Excited by their progress, Larry and Sergey offered BackRub to the Stanford community on a trial basis. The university had a large server (a computer that stores codes for websites) to meet the needs of faculty and students. Anyone who logged on to Stanford.edu could use BackRub to find information on the World Wide Web. The first users quickly shared their satisfaction with others. BackRub acquired a reputation as an effective tool.

A Snappy Name

Larry and Sergey felt their search tool deserved a more exciting name than BackRub. They wanted something simple but snappy—a name that people would remember. Stumped, they sought help from their

IN FOCUS

Clients and Servers

Generally, two types of computers interact when someone accesses the Internet. Most people have what is called a client computer. These computers contain one of a number of special programs known as browsers. Browsers allow a computer user to see what is available on the World Wide Web, but they do not store Web pages themselves. Each site on the Web has a unique address known as a uniform resource locater (URL). Using a special protocol (series of steps), the client computer requests a particular URL from the server. The most widely used protocol is http (hypertext transfer protocol), which was written by the inventor of the World Wide Web, Tim Berners-Lee.

Servers are high-memory computers that contain information codes for large numbers of websites. They also use http (or another protocol) to send requested websites to the client computer. Using this system, Stanford's large server made BackRub available to client computers all over the university.

A domain name is a website's unique identity. No two sites can have the same name. Google's domain name is www.google.com.

office mates. The brainstorming sessions that ensued lasted several days. "No, no, no," Larry vetoed suggestion after suggestion. He began to doubt they would ever find the right name.

"How about Googleplex?" asked office mate Sean Anderson at last. He thought the name fit because a googolplex is a huge number—one followed by one hundred zeroes. Larry and Sergey's search engine would handle huge amounts of data. The name Googolplex seemed to say that there was no limit to the amount of information it could process.

Larry liked the idea. "How about we try Google?" he suggested. The shortened term also indicates a vast number.

A quick check by Sean revealed that Google had not been registered as an Internet domain name. Within several hours, Larry had officially taken the name for their search engine. The next day Sean realized that the real word was not *g-o-o-g-l-e* but *g-o-o-g-o-l*. If he had spelled the word correctly, he would have found it already taken as a domain name. Sean's spelling mistake had been fortunate indeed!

More and more computers: As Sergey and Larry used their program to index new websites, their computer needs grew.

"A Web in Your Pocket"

As more people at Stanford tried Google, its database continued to expand. The popular search engine constantly indexed and added new websites. All this growth meant that Larry and Sergey needed more computers to store information and to process requests. Neither young man was wealthy. Where would the new computers come from?

Larry and Sergey solved the problem by buying inexpensive electronic components and building their own computers. They also scouted out the loading dock where computers were delivered to the university. Occasionally they would find a computer or two just lying around. "We would just borrow a few machines," admitted Larry, "figuring if they didn't pick it up right away, they didn't need it so badly."

Soon their office in the Gates Building was filled with computers. And still they needed more space—and computers. So they began stacking the computers one on top of another in Larry's dorm room. Sergey's room became their business office as Google continued to grow. Their professors helped with funding by awarding them ten thousand dollars from the Stanford Digital Libraries Project. But they still needed more money. According to Larry, they "maxed out three credit cards buying hard disks off the back of a truck." They borrowed credit cards from

IN FOCUS

Big Claims

Within two years of beginning their research, Larry and Sergey were ready to make big claims for Google. In April 1998, they published a paper titled "Anatomy of a Large Scale Hypertextual Web Search Engine." They explained why Google was better than any other search engine. They noted that the World Wide Web was growing at an amazing rate. But Google's crawler worked so rapidly and efficiently that users could count on finding the most recent Web pages among their search results.

Users could also be certain of finding the most relevant items toward the front of the list. "We want our notion of 'relevance' to only include the very best documents," they wrote, "since there may be tens of thousands of slightly relevant documents." Although many papers have been written about search engines, their document is the one most cited by other authors.

their parents. And when they thought about all the money they were spending, they felt "like a sidewalk worm during a rainstorm."

A Business or Great Research?

Despite their financial distress, Larry and Sergey believed there was a bright future for Google. Users at Stanford liked it. The two felt certain it would prove popular elsewhere too. If they could license Google (sell the use of its technology to an established computer company), they could solve their two problems. They would have plenty of money, and Google would get the following it deserved. But Larry and Sergey could not find a company willing to license Google—at least not at the price they were asking. Larry valued Google's worth at $1.6 million.

For eighteen months, the hopeful computer engineers sought to interest Internet companies. They gave demonstrations all over Silicon Valley and explained why their search engine was superior to others. Although many people found the presentation fascinating, no one considered a better search engine important. Internet companies (often called portals) concentrated on other features, such as e-mail or news services. Even Jerry Yang and David Filo, the founders of a search engine called Yahoo, did not think that Google posed a threat to them. They suggested that

Competition?: Jerry Yang *(left)* and David Filo *(right)*, founders of the search engine Yahoo, suggested that Larry and Sergey start their own business.

Larry and Sergey start their own business. The disappointed young men felt reluctant to take such a step.

"Have Fun and Keep Googling"

Eager for feedback from their loyal Stanford users, Larry and Sergey compiled a list of "Google Friends" and sent an e-mail asking them for "comments, criticisms, bugs, ideas." They kept improving the Google home page. They added a short description for each result that Google returned. The descriptions helped users evaluate at a glance whether or not a particular website was worth investigating. In July 1998, they announced that their index contained 24 million Web pages. And it kept on growing. "Have fun and keep googling," Larry and Sergey urged their friends.

All over campus, students and faculty did. Google grew so fast that soon it was receiving more than ten thousand requests a day. Larry and Sergey needed even more computers and more space. They were also taking up too much of the university's computer resources at standford.edu. Once so many people used Google at the same time, that Stanford's computer network had crashed. It was time to move Google off campus. That would mean starting a company. But Larry and Sergey badly wanted to earn their degrees. They weren't certain what to do. "You guys can always come back and finish your PhD's if you don't succeed," Professor Jeffrey Ullman advised them. The open-door policy convinced them to give the business world a try.

"The Single Best Idea I Have Heard in Years"

Luckily one of Larry's professors, David Cheriton, knew a wealthy investor. Andy von Bechtolsheim, a Stanford graduate, had cofounded Sun Microsystems, a multimillion-dollar company specializing in computers, software, and information technology. Cheriton told Larry and Sergey that they should speak to Bechtolsheim about Google.

Late one night, Sergey e-mailed Bechtolsheim. Almost immediately a reply bounced back. Bechtolsheim wanted to know more about their search engine. He suggested that they meet at eight thirty the next morning at David Cheriton's house. Excited, hopeful, maybe a little nervous, Larry and Sergey waited on their professor's porch at the appointed time. Without even entering the house, Bechtolsheim opened his laptop and allowed the eager pair to show him what Google could do. Its speed and relevant results impressed Bechtolsheim greatly. He asked lots of questions and approved their plan to build inex-

Google is a go: Sergey *(left)* and Larry *(right)* made the tough decision to try to start a company instead of finishing their graduate work.

pensive computers themselves instead of buying the latest (and highest priced) technology to store their database.

But Bechtolsheim had little time to spare. "This is the single best idea I have heard in years," he said at last. "I want to be part of it." Even though Larry and Sergey hadn't started their company yet, he proposed writing a check at once.

The astonished students had not expected such a rapid response. How much money could they request? Hurriedly they discussed the matter while Bechtolsheim returned to his car for his checkbook.

Soon Larry and Sergey had another surprise. "Oh, I don't think that's enough," Bechtolsheim replied to their suggestion of fifty thousand dollars. "I think it should be twice that amount."

Dumbfounded, Larry and Sergey accepted a check for one hundred thousand dollars. They celebrated their windfall with a big breakfast at Burger King. For two weeks, the check lay in Larry's desk drawer while he and Sergey went about establishing their company and opening a bank account. By September 7, 1998, the paperwork was complete. Google Inc. officially became a company. Larry, as chief executive officer, and Sergey, as president, hired another Stanford student, Craig Silverstein, to work for them.

As a growing company, Google no longer fit conveniently in Larry's dorm room. So the new businessmen rented a garage from a young woman they knew, Susan Wojcicki. They stocked their new office with food and transferred all their computers. The crowded garage also held three tables, three chairs, a folded-up Ping-Pong table, and

Google office: For their first office space, Larry and Sergey rented the garage of Susan Wojcicki in Menlo Park, California.

desks made of sturdy wooden doors atop sawhorses. The garage door was usually open so that fresh air could circulate.

These were exciting, exhausting days for Larry and Sergey. Often it was well past midnight when they left for the night. Their only transportation was Craig's car, which backfired loudly, "like a machine gun going off." Trying not to waken Susan, they pushed Craig's noisy car out of the driveway and into the street before starting it.

"You Have to Index the Entire Web"

Just two weeks after Google's establishment as a commercial business, Larry and Sergey were back in the classroom, speaking to members of Stanford's computer department. They titled their talk "Google and the WebBase: What Can You Do with a

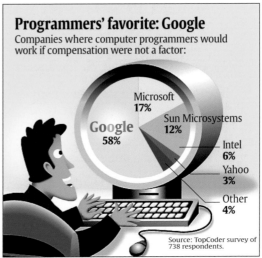

USA TODAY Snapshots®

Programmers' favorite: Google

Companies where computer programmers would work if compensation were not a factor:

Google 58%
Microsoft 17%
Sun Microsystems 12%
Intel 6%
Yahoo 3%
Other 4%

Source: TopCoder survey of 738 respondents.

By Jae Yang and Bob Laird, USA TODAY, 2005

Web in Your Pocket?" Sergey wasted little time in letting everyone know. "I'm Sergey Brin and that's Larry over there. I'm going to jump right into it here," he announced casually. First, he demonstrated that Google worked better than other search engines. Then he explained why. "Let me tell you what the challenges are of a search engine," he continued. "You have to index the entire Web." The work was never finished because the Web was growing and changing every day.

But Google was clearly up to the task. Larry explained that their crawler downloaded about one hundred Web pages every second.

IN FOCUS

Just the Right Time

Craig Silverstein believes Larry and Sergey started Google in exactly the right window of time. Even a year before Google was founded, the World Wide Web was relatively small. A person who conducted a search on a particular topic would not receive a large number of results. He or she could easily review the entire list. One search engine would serve the purpose as well as any other. After 1998, however, it was a different story. The Web had been growing at a phenomenal rate. Searching a topic produced an enormous list. People no longer had the time to explore every Web listing. They needed a search engine that would do the work for them by putting the most relevant websites at the top of the list. According to Craig, that's exactly what Google did.

First employee: Craig Silverstein *(shown here in 2008)* was the first person Sergey and Larry hired.

Google continued to grow in two ways. It indexed more Web pages, and more people began using it. Larry and Sergey had no need to advertise. Their search engine was so good that the number of users multiplied rapidly. Soon Google was processing one hundred thousand search requests a day. Within months, *PC Magazine* included it in its list of the Top 100 Web Sites and Search Engines for 1998. Larry and Sergey continued to pour all their energy into making Google even better.

Creating a logo: As their computer company grew, Larry and Sergey moved into offices in Palo Alto, California. Next on the list was coming up with a logo.

"All the Information in the World"

■ ■ ■ ■

Larry and Sergey kept building computers and downloading the Web. They hired more people. Soon Susan's garage could no longer contain their growing business. Finding larger quarters, Larry and Sergey moved their office to Palo Alto. As the company grew, so did their need for more funding. Google had become popular enough to attract the attention of top investors in Silicon Valley. Two firms, Kleiner Perkins and Sequoia Capital, decided to invest in Google. Each of them put up $12.5 million. Larry and Sergey were thrilled. Once again, they celebrated with their favorite fast food at Burger King.

Later, in a press statement, Larry spoke of Google's plans "to continue to provide the best search experience on the Web." Sergey took the promise a step further. "A perfect search engine will process and understand all the information in the world," he declared. "That is where Google is headed."

There was only one drawback to Larry and Sergey's profitable deal. Executives from both investment firms wanted Larry and Sergey to hire a new CEO—someone older and more experienced who would ensure Google made money. So far, the search engine hadn't brought in any revenue at all. Larry and Sergey did not charge people for using Google, and they didn't know yet how Google would make money. In spite of this, they were not eager to hire a CEO. They liked controlling their company and didn't want anyone else telling them what to do. But dutifully they began considering candidates for the job.

 Almost from the beginning, Google provided a pet-friendly environment for its employees. Its online listing of Google milestones notes that Yoshka, the first "company dog," came to work with Urs Hoelzle, senior vice president of operations, in April 1999.

A Playful Logo

Finding the right person for another position had proved much easier. One month earlier, in May 1999, Larry and Sergey had hired their former landlady, Susan Wojcicki, to take charge of marketing.

www.usatoday.com

USA TODAY

Money

SECTION B

Google   Google   Google

Google   Google

July 5, 2007

The house that helped build Google

From the Pages of
USA TODAY

Mountain View, Calif.—Susan Wojcicki is reminiscing about her old home in Menlo Park, Calif.

"It's a very humble house, less than 2,000 square feet [185 square meters]," she recalls fondly. A cozy, four-bedroom home—and incredibly historic.

After earning her MBA in 1998, Wojcicki bought 232 Santa Margarita Ave. for about $600,000. She rented the garage to two Stanford students for $1,700 a month to help with the mortgage. The renters: no ordinary slackers, but the Google Guys, Larry Page and Sergey Brin, who incubated Google right there.

"It's a good reminder for the company that we did come from a small house, not a fancy house," says Wojcicki.

Her life-changing decision to open her home to Brin and Page did more than just help start the world's most-popular search engine. It also landed Wojcicki a key early job at Google less than a year after purchasing the home. Today, she's one of its top-ranked executives, overseeing the crucial online advertising business as vice president of project management.

"There are no sets of words that can be used to describe Susan's contribution to the company," says Google CEO Eric Schmidt. "She's historic in terms of our company's founding. She's also one of those people who thinks very broadly and quickly, and (it's) deceiving because she's so pleasant."

In Google's fledgling days, Wojcicki . . . was in charge of marketing efforts. Brin and Page charged her with spreading the word about Google on a shoestring. Her big idea: stir word-of-mouth by putting Google's search engine all over the Web. She reached out to companies to license Google search for their websites and offered it free to universities.

Meanwhile, the humble house where Google was incubated was purchased by Google in September. Google won't disclose how much it paid, but homes in the neighborhood sell for more than $1 million. "I haven't had time to think about what we'll do with it," says CEO Schmidt. "But I figured we should buy it soon rather than later."

—Jefferson Graham

Part of her job was to make Google attractive to as many people as possible. One way to do this, she decided, was to create an appealing logo. Larry and Sergey took a keen interest in the logo. They imagined something distinctive but lively. And they thought they knew just the person to design what they wanted.

From landlady to Google marketer: Sergey and Larry hired Susan Wojcicki *(above)* to work on marketing their new company. Wojcicki had previously rented them her garage to use as their first office.

Ruth Kedar was an Israeli graphic designer at Stanford. Larry and Sergey met her in 1999 through a mutual friend. They were impressed with her sketches and hired her to design the logo. Kedar based her logo on an earlier drawing of Sergey's, making several sets of changes. In one early sketch, Ruth turned an *o* into a smiley face. In another, the *o* became a magnifying glass to stress the thorough nature of Google searches. And in still another, Kedar turned an *o* into a bull's-eye to show that Google searches were right on target. Eventually the artist and the founders decided on the bold printing and bright colors that have become familiar all over the world. The simple, playful image conveys an important message: a Google search is easy, it brings good results, and it is fun.

Burning Man

In August 1999, Google users noticed a change in the usual logo. The second *o* had been turned into a stick figure. Most people would have

Logo Art

The Burning Man stick figure on the Google logo marked the beginning of a cherished tradition. That November a turkey logo appeared for Thanksgiving. And the next October, Sergey, in a burst of playfulness, made the o's in Google into pumpkins. "We should show people in the world that people at Google care about Halloween," he declared. User response was so positive that Google began featuring other special logos for holidays and events.

been puzzled. But those who knew Larry and Sergey read a secret message. The stick figure stood for Burning Man, an annual festival held in the Black Rock Desert of Nevada. That's exactly where Larry and Sergey were heading for a much-needed break. The offbeat event was somewhat reminiscent of the hippie gatherings of the 1960s. It appealed to Larry's and Sergey's creative spirits and inclination to do things their own way.

For a week, the hardworking Google founders lived without cell phones or computers. They camped out in a temporary city built by the eighteen thousand people gathering in the desert. They prepared their own food and mingled with people from all walks of life, from clowns to other computer folks. Instead of being tied to a schedule, they could eat and sleep whenever they felt like it. Larry and Sergey enjoyed Burning Man so much that they decided to return to the festival every year.

Rapid Growth

Energized by their unique experience, Larry and Sergey returned to Palo Alto ready to address the growing demands on their search engine. That meant buying more computers to hold their expanding database and to process search requests. But even with their recent influx of funds, they

By September 1999, Google was processing three and a half million searches each day, sometimes sixty-five per second.

needed to be thrifty. Instead of buying costly, high-quality computer systems, Larry and Sergey went bargain shopping. And they continued their hands-on approach to Google. Purchasing inexpensive PCs and disks, they rebuilt them to suit their needs. Special software and wiring connected the computers so they operated as a single system. When one computer failed, the software eliminated it from the circuit. That way it wouldn't bring down the whole system. Within one month, the number of Google's computers jumped from three hundred to two thousand.

IN FOCUS

Server Farms

The computers on which Google stores the World Wide Web are not located in its comfortable company headquarters. By 2005 Google had an estimated half million computers. These are located in dozens of data centers all over the world called server farms. Not much different from any inexpensive PC, the server computers are stacked in tall metal racks.

When someone makes a Google request, special software sends it to a cluster of computers. Hundreds or thousands of computers review the request instantaneously, comparing words in the search box with Google's vast index. Then the software gathers the responses and ranks them. The procedure involves "tens of billions of cycles" and "hundreds of megabytes" of data. But in less than one second, the user receives the results on his or her home computer.

Hungry Computer Engineers

As they expanded their computer network, Larry and Sergey were also adjusting to new company quarters. After only six months in their Palo Alto office, Google had needed more space, so they moved to offices in Mountain View, California. There, they were determined to provide the best possible work environment for their forty employees. That included the best possible food. For some time, Larry and Sergey had been seeking a gourmet chef. They gave twenty-five top chefs a chance to try out by cooking a meal for their employees. But none of them satisfied their demanding tastes. Finally, in November 1999, Charlie Ayers took the job, and a Google institution was born. Charlie's Place, as the cafeteria would come to be known, served food that was healthy, delicious, and free. People could eat there for breakfast, lunch,

Google chef: Larry and Sergey hired Charlie Ayers *(shown above in 2008)* to be the chef at the cafeteria at Google headquarters. Ayers left Google in 2006 to start his own restaurant in Palo Alto, California.

Mentalplex

Larry and Sergey find it hard to resist a good joke. In 2000 Google users received instructions about a new technique called mentalplex. A spinning red and blue circle appeared on their computer screens. Users were told to focus on the circle without moving their heads. They were to project their search request mentally onto the swirling disk. Google was supposed to respond directly to their thoughts! Confidence in Google ran so high that some people may have actually tried the procedure. Those who remembered the date probably just laughed. It was April 1. Mentalplex was merely the first of many April Fool's pranks to come.

and dinner. They never knew what tempting treats Charlie would dish out from "organic tofu mushroom ragout" to the "buttermilk fried chicken Elvis loved."

Major Milestones

The new millennium brought some exciting changes to the company. In May 2000, it released ten foreign language versions of Google.com. The next month, it teamed up with the search engine, Yahoo. Just a few years earlier, when Larry and Sergey were students, Yahoo had declined to license their technology. At this time, Google would be handling some of Yahoo's search requests. By June its index had grown to one billion Web pages. It processed eighteen million searches each day. That made Google the largest search engine in the world. "You can search the equivalent of a stack of paper more than seventy miles [113 kilometers] high in less than half a second," Larry Page declared. "We think that's pretty cool."

Becoming businessmen: Sergey *(left)* and Larry *(right)* first introduced ads to the Google website in 2000. They were trying to figure out a way for the company to make money.

"Don't Be Evil"

Larry and Sergey were computer engineers before they were businessmen. Fascinated by technology, they had no idea how Google was going to make money. People did not have to pay to use Google, and Larry and Sergey did not like the idea of selling ads to bring in money. But they knew they had to generate a healthy income to pay their employees, to keep Google running, and to provide a return to their investors. Despite their initial hesitations, they finally decided to experiment cautiously with ads. The placement of an ad would be based on its relevance to a particular search query. "Our theory was, well, we'll try this for a little while," Larry recalled later.

AdWords

When Google presented its first ads in January 2000, the results were disappointing. Google continued to attract lots of users, but the company wasn't making as much money with the advertising as Larry and Sergey had hoped. Then, in the spring, the stock market crashed. Businesses had less money to spend on advertising. Even as other Silicon Valley companies floundered, however, Google continued to grow. As a private company, its fortunes were not tied to the stock market. Larry and Sergey hired many talented computer engineers who had been laid off by other companies. They moved Google to bigger offices in Mountain View.

Despite its expansion, Google still lacked a successful advertising mode. Susan Wojcicki took the lead in improving the previous approach. The new service, AdWords was introduced in October 2000

AdSense

In March 2003, Google launched AdSense, which offered a way for websites to make money. Websites that signed up for AdSense were scanned so that appropriate ads could be placed on them. Advertisers paid Google for every time someone clicked onto their ad. Google shared half the proceeds with the websites. Internet expert and writer Danny Sullivan told *USA Today* that AdSense "basically turned the Web into a giant Google billboard. It effectively meant that Google could turn everyone's content into a place for Google ads."

Endless Supply of Doodles

Google is about fun as well as information. Google doodles combine both. For almost two years after the first doodle on the Google logo, Larry and Sergey hired someone outside the company to create the whimsical drawings that Google users enjoyed.

Dennis Hwang, an artist and computer engineer who worked for Google, was given the task of sharpening the doodles and putting them online. Dennis was good at tweaking the imaginative drawings in just the right way. A doodle he altered for Bastille Day (French Independence Day) caught Larry's and Sergey's attention. Delighted with his talent, they made Dennis the official Google doodler in 2000.

Since then Dennis, who loves his work, has done about fifty doodles a year. Some celebrate holidays, others the birthdays of famous people or the anniversaries of historic events. People can click onto the doodle to see exactly what is being celebrated.

Google doodles: Dennis Hwang poses with one of his doodles for Google in 2002.

Larry and Sergey have the final say on all doodles. In an official Google blog, Dennis wrote, "Holding up my mockups and holding my breath while Larry and Sergey do their thumbs-up, thumbs-down, emperor things is never boring, and I love the fact that my little niche within this company has turned out to be something so cool and creative and well, Google-y."

on Google's home page. As before, the placement of an ad would depend on each particular search query. For example, if someone typed "piano" into Google, she might see ads for sheet music, piano lessons, or other musical instruments. She would not find ads for cosmetics, bicycles, or algebra tutoring. All ads were dubbed "sponsored links" and were carefully separated from the regular search engine results. In this first version of Adwords, advertisers paid Google according to the number of times their ads appeared. "Have a credit card and 5 minutes?" potential customers read. "Get your ad on Google today." Many businesspeople decided to take advantage of the speed and convenience of placing their ads on Google. Soon Google was generating a very healthy income. Larry and Sergey believed that the right ad in the right place at the right time could be as helpful to the person doing the search as it was to the business doing the advertising.

Another Kind of Search

Meanwhile, Larry and Sergey had another issue to address. They had promised their financial backers that they would hire an experienced businessperson to be CEO. But the young founders weren't eager to bring in a newcomer who might try to tell them what to do. By early 2001, Larry and Sergey had interviewed about seventy-five candidates. None of them seemed right for the job. Google's backers were becoming anxious.

Then Eric Schmidt arrived to talk with them. Schmidt wasn't really interested in computer search, and at the age of forty-six, he considered twenty-seven-year-olds Larry and Sergey mere kids. But John Doerr, one of Google's backers, convinced Schmidt to accept Sergey's invitation for an interview.

When Schmidt arrived at the office Larry and Sergey shared, he found himself facing his own biography, blown up large and projected onto a wall. Even bigger surprises were in store. Whatever Schmidt said, it seemed that Larry and Sergey challenged him. It was almost like a replay of the young founders' initial meeting in San Francisco, when they had argued with each other so eagerly. "They criticized every single technical point I made, and everything I was doing in my business," Schmidt later recalled. At that time, his company, Novell, was working on a plan aimed at improving the Internet. "They argued that this was the stupidest thing they'd ever heard of," continued Schmidt. "I was just floored. It was really arrogant."

Very few people had dared confront Schmidt the way Larry and Sergey did. Thinking back over the meeting, however, Schmidt was more intrigued than insulted.

Despite their arguing, Larry and Sergey looked favorably on Eric. They appreciated the fact that he had a science as well as a business background. Eric held a PhD from the University of California at Berkeley's School of Engineering. He had held high-ranking positions at two major IT (information technology) companies. On top of all this, he had attended the Burning Man festival. That was a definite plus with Larry and Sergey.

When the Google founders finally offered him a position, Eric accepted. The idea of working for a smaller company that was doing exciting things appealed to him.

Eric joined Google as chairman of the board of directors in March 2001. Five months later, in August, he was named CEO. Larry and Sergey took on new positions. Larry became president of products, and Sergey became president of technology.

New CEO: Eric Schmidt became Google's CEO in 2001. He had previous experience at two other information technology companies.

Expanding the Web

The World Wide Web provides vast resources to the public, but Larry and Sergey recognize its limits. The same month that Eric Schmidt joined Google, the two founders gave a talk at the Commonwealth Club of California in San Francisco. Stressing that most of the world's information was not available on the Web, Larry said, "You can't access content that's in libraries. You can't access magazines. You can't access newspapers, in general, or old newspaper content. You can't access all the television programs that have ever been broadcast. Then Larry made a bold prediction. "But all these things will happen." Clearly, Google was gearing up for another seemingly impossible task.

Company Motto

"The place was always a zoo," Schmidt said about the atmosphere he found when he started work at Google. But it was a creative, productive zoo. By the middle of 2001, Larry and Sergey had hired more than two hundred employees. They called themselves Googlers. Every week new people came on board. How would this galloping expansion affect the company? To preserve Google's distinct identity, Larry and Sergey held a meeting of about a dozen long-term employees. As ideas and guiding principles were brought forth, an engineer named Paul Buchheit decided to simplify them. "All of these things can be covered by just saying, 'Don't be evil,'" he said.

The words seemed to resonate with his fellow Googlers. One, Amit Patel, liked the motto so much that he copied it on nearly all the whiteboards scattered throughout the headquarters. Other people remembered and liked the motto. Larry and Sergey thought it captured the essence of the company. They always wanted Google to put its mission ahead of profits. "Don't be evil" became famous as Google's official slogan.

Always Something New

There seemed no end to Larry and Sergey's energy. They made Google available in twenty-six languages. They opened their first international office in Tokyo, Japan. They launched Image Search, which allows users to look through photos and pictures. "If one picture is worth 1,000 words, what about a million pictures?" they asked. "Or to be more precise, 250 million pictures?" The number boggled the imagination. No other search engine could boast a collection anywhere near that size. Larry and Sergey oversaw every aspect of Google's widening operations, from hiring to offering new services to checking out the doodles for the logo. According to one top computer scientist, nothing got done without their okay.

Taking Risks

Larry and Sergey believe it is more important to try out new ideas than to play it safe in business. Sometimes this philosophy can cost them money. When one Google official told Larry about a mistake that cost the company several million dollars, Larry was philosophical. "We'll know better next time," he said. "But, oh, by the way, it's good that you made this mistake. I'm glad because we need to be the kind of company that is willing to make mistakes. Because if we're not willing to make mistakes, then we're not taking risks. And if we're not taking risks, we won't get to the next level."

A Great Place to Work

Google's founders understood that play can be as important as work. They liked to have fun, and they knew their employees were more efficient when they had fun too. Depending on their schedules, Googlers could join a game of football, roller hockey, or beach volleyball during work hours. They could hop aboard a scooter and speed through the courtyard at headquarters. Google headquarters also boasted workout equipment, a hair

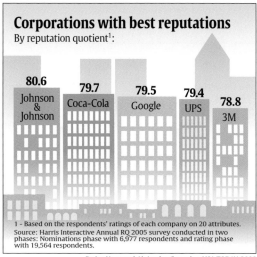

USA TODAY Snapshots®

Corporations with best reputations
By reputation quotient[1]:

80.6 Johnson & Johnson
79.7 Coca-Cola
79.5 Google
79.4 UPS
78.8 3M

1 - Based on the respondents' ratings of each company on 20 attributes.
Source: Harris Interactive Annual RQ 2005 survey conducted in two phases: Nominations phase with 6,977 respondents and rating phase with 19,564 respondents.

By Jae Yang and Alejandro Gonzalez, USA TODAY, 2006

salon, a laundry, and a car wash, as well as medical and dental facilities. But if Larry and Sergey had made the Google work environment just about perfect, that wasn't enough for them. What about the hour-long commute to and from San Francisco, where many Googlers lived? Eventually Larry and Sergey hired a bus with wireless Internet service. Googlers not only got free rides, but they also got to use their laptops. Not surprisingly, Google was listed as one of the "100 Best Companies to work for" by *Fortune* magazine.

Outside of work, Larry and Sergey lived simply. Their apartments weren't luxurious, and they didn't drive expensive cars. They dressed casually—especially Sergey, who liked to wear shorts and T-shirts. Both young men liked to date. Larry once joked that Google finally started making money because Sergey wanted to make a bigger impression on

January 9, 2002

Visit to Google's HQ provides blast from Silicon Valley past

From the Pages of
USA TODAY

MOUNTAIN VIEW, Calif. —Whoa, is this a time warp or what?

I'm in Google's headquarters, otherwise known as the Googleplex, and it's sooo old-time Silicon Valley. By that, I mean the 1970s and 1980s, when technology companies could still be counterculture and cute and full of people who thought they could change the world before dinner.

Privately held Google runs a search engine. It's one of the most beloved entities on the Internet and one of the few pure-Internet firms that's profitable. Google is so fast and accurate, it is used by millions of viewers of *Who Wants To Be A Millionaire*. Google's statistics show spikes in usage after each question.

So I came here to see what magic goes on inside the Googleplex. . . .

Scooters lean against walls. Big exercise balls are everywhere. Walk around and you'll see piles of roller hockey equipment, random toys, a bin offering 13 kinds of cereal including Lucky Charms, a wall mural of the company's history done in crayon, a spalike room marked by a sign that says "Googlers massaged here" and a cafeteria where gourmet meals are served by the former chef for the Grateful Dead.

The place is crawling with twentysomething engineers who apparently prepare for work by dressing in the dark. All 280 employees went to see *Harry Potter and the*

the women he asked out. But neither one cared about profits nearly as much as they cared about making Google an even better experience for everyone. They had long outgrown their initial tendency to argue with each other. Larry once estimated that they agree two-thirds of

Sorcerer's Stone together.

The quirkiness flows from the top. Google was founded by one guy who once built an inkjet printer out of Legos and another who hails from Moscow and studies trapeze.

As I'm getting to know Google, in walks Eric Schmidt, Google's CEO. The time warp seems complete. Schmidt, 46, has been around since the actual old days. He was Sun Microsystems' chief technology officer, then CEO of Novell. In

Game room: A Google employee plays the piano in the company's headquarters in 2002.

August, he joined Google. "It's a way of getting lots of praise," Schmidt says wryly. . . .

Schmidt first met Page and Brin casually, and they argued with him for 90 minutes about the architecture of the Internet. "That's MY expertise," Schmidt says with mock disdain. "How could THEY argue with ME?"

Schmidt outwardly looks like he's having fun. So what if he has to manage a culture that is . . . almost unmanageable? And so he might be a little old for scooters and Lucky Charms and parking lot roller hockey.

"This is a blast," Schmidt says. "I want to hang out with 27-year-olds the rest of my life."

Before I leave, Schmidt offers me a souvenir. Lots of companies have given me logo T-shirts, baseball hats and coffee mugs. But this is a first. He hands me a pair of Google boxer shorts.

—Kevin Maney

the time. Sergey put the figure at 80 to 90 percent. "If we both feel the same way," Larry said, "we're probably right. If we don't agree, it's probably a toss-up." Perhaps with a hint of mischief, he added, "If we both agree and nobody else agrees with us, we assume we're right!"

USA TODAY

CHAPTER EIGHT

9/11: After the terrorist attacks on the World Trade Center in New York City and the Pentagon (*above*) near Washington, D.C., on September 11, 2001, people used Google to get to news stories and make donations to victims.

Branching Out in All Directions

On September 11, 2001, the entire world mourned the loss of life in the terrorist attacks on the World Trade Center in New York City and on the Pentagon near Washington, D.C. Television coverage was continuous. But in the aftermath of the tragedies, people also turned to the Internet for information. Many individuals were unable to access such popular sources as CNN.com or the *New York Times* website due to the huge demand. Google copied and stored top stories from these sites. When people couldn't get through to the actual news sources, they could follow a link from Google to one of its special caches (pockets) of information.

Within days Google had a link on its home page that offered additional links to news stories and support services such as the Red Cross and sites where donations could be made for the 9/11 victims. Author Richard W. Wiggins wrote not long after the disaster, "By meeting user demand for trusted information sources related to September 11, Google has trained millions of people to expect Google.com to deliver breaking news." In the following weeks and months, Larry, Sergey, and Eric Schmidt decided to continue Google's vital role. When they officially launched Google News one year after the attacks, it featured four thousand news sources. People continued to flock to Google for the breaking national and world developments.

And Google continued to grow at a dizzying pace.

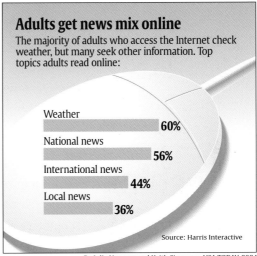

USA TODAY Snapshots®

Adults get news mix online

The majority of adults who access the Internet check weather, but many seek other information. Top topics adults read online:

Weather **60%**

National news **56%**

International news **44%**

Local news **36%**

Source: Harris Interactive

By Julia Neyman and Keith Simmons, USA TODAY, 2004

Several months before the introduction of Google News, Larry, Sergey, and Eric entered into an important agreement with America Online (AOL). The deal gave 34 million users of CompuServe, Netscape, and AOL.com access to Google search and to its ads. The next year saw the opening of Google's first office in Australia. Barely five years old, Google was coming to dominate the search market.

By 2003 the word *google* had become a verb. When people wanted to do research on a topic, they "Googled it." In January the American Dialect Society voted it the "most useful" Word of the Year for 2002.

"You Have to Be a Little Silly"

September 2003 found Larry and Sergey traveling through Israel and Europe. They were thinking of opening new international offices and scouting out possible future employees. One of their stops was an Israeli high school for mathematically gifted students, where they received a rousing welcome. Jumping right into their talk, speaking casually as if to old friends, Larry told of his "crazy idea" to download the Web on his computer. "You have to be a little silly about the goals you are going to set," he explained. "You should try to do things most people would not."

Many young people in the audience had been born in the Soviet Union/Russia and had immigrated to Israel with their parents. Sergey surprised and delighted them by speaking some sentences in Russian. Then he continued, "I was told that your school recently got seven out of the top ten places in a math competition throughout all Israel."

Ignorant of Sergey's mischievous humor and showmanship, the students clapped for their accomplishment. "What I have to say," added Sergey, "is in the words of my father, 'What about the other three?'" Immediately the applause turned to laughter.

Toward the end of their presentation, Larry and Sergey noticed a shift in the students' attention. Everyone was turning toward the back of the room. It took a moment for the startled young men on-stage to realize that former Soviet prime minister Mikhail Gorbachev and Israeli leader Shimon Peres had just entered the auditorium.

After addressing the students and saying a few good things about Google's founders, Gorbachev shook their hands. Larry and Sergey's school visit had ended on a political note that neither could have possibly imagined.

Google and books: Google vice president of search products, Marissa Mayer, speaks to the press about Google making book excerpts available to be searched online.

Google's Moon Shot

Toward the end of 2003, Larry and Sergey unveiled an ambitious new program they dubbed Google Print. The goal was to scan and index every book, both current and out of print— every book in the entire world. Marissa Mayer, a vice president at Google, once called the book project "our moon shot." She was comparing the tremendous task Google faced with the challenge President John Kennedy set in 1961 of landing a man on the moon. Like Kennedy, Google gave itself a deadline of ten years. The odds against both enterprises were overwhelming. But the United States achieved Kennedy's goal with the first lunar landing in 1969. Google intended to reach its goal too.

Meanwhile, the World Wide Web continued to expand. Google kept pace with its astronomical rate of growth. By February 2004, Google's index contained 6 billion items. This total included Web pages and images, as well as a growing number of book items from the Google Print project. Still in an experimental stage, this service did not provide complete copies of books. Google did not want to infringe on the rights of the authors or publishers. But viewers could see first chapters, snippets of information, and reviews. They could also click onto a link to purchase books.

A New Googleplex

In the summer of 2003, Google moved its eight hundred-plus employees to larger, fancier accommodations in Mountain View. To many people, the new location, called the Googleplex, seemed more like a college campus than a corporate headquarters. Larry took the lead in designing informal, creative work spaces for employees. Through the years, he had visited many offices throughout the world. Whenever he saw something he especially liked, he would whip out his camera and take a picture.

The Googleplex: Google moved to new, larger headquarters in 2003.

August 26, 2003

The search engine that could

From the Pages of
<u>USA TODAY</u>

MOUNTAIN VIEW, Calif. —Susan Wojcicki remembers when two Stanford students came to rent room in her . . . [garage] in September 1998 for a new dot-com enterprise.

It was a system for searching the Internet, one that they claimed was more effective than any other. "My reaction was, 'OK, good luck. The rent's $1,700 a month, and don't forget to separate the recycling,'" she says.

Larry Page and Sergey Brin and their brainstorm, Google, quickly outgrew her home. Today, the founders and their landlady—who wound up quitting her job at Intel to join the boys—are in different wings of the four-building sprawling campus known as the Googleplex, a 1,000-employee paradise with free food, unlimited ice cream, pool and Ping-Pong tables and complementary massages, plus the ability to spend 20% of work time on any outside activity. "They built Google to be their dream environment," Wojcicki says.

Overall, Google "represents 75% of all searches," says Danny Sullivan, editor of the *Search Engine Watch* online newsletter (searchenginewatch.com). "It's gotten to the point where people think if it's not in Google, it doesn't exist."

Today, millions Google themselves, friends, blind dates, employers and employees. Students wait till the last minute to Google assignments. Shoppers Google products and prices before purchasing. One columnist suggested that Google is so vital in our lives that it's a deity of sorts, everywhere and all-knowing.

As Google prepares to celebrate its fifth anniversary Sept. 7, it's expanding beyond basic searches. Google now embraces comparison shopping, news, the personal online journals called Weblogs and even a service that blocks pesky pop-up ads. It answers 200 million search requests a day—more than 2,300 every second—in 88 languages. It indexes 3.1 billion Web pages with the help of 10,000 supercomputers.

The aim: to organize the world's information.

—Jefferson Graham

Wonderful Work Environment

By 2009 the Googleplex included more than 3 million square feet (280,000 sq. m) in thirty buildings. Employees used bicycles, in-line skates, and electric scooters to navigate the spacious grounds. Inside, huge medicine balls, pool tables, lava lamps (a Google trademark) massage chairs, snack racks, and sleep pads kept life convenient and fun for everyone.

Larry and Sergey's shared office at the Googleplex reveals their interests as well as their accessibility. Without secretaries to help structure their day, they are free to set their own agendas. The office features two staircases, a glassed-in loft where they work, and giant computer screens. For recreation there is a massage chair and fitness equipment. Prominently displayed, a space suit bears Sergey's name—a reflection of his future plans to venture into space.

New digs: Sergey *(left)* and Larry *(right)* pose in their new headquarters in 2004.

Larry wanted people to feel at home at work. He believed that sharing space encouraged people to work together and exchange ideas. "We spent a lot of time getting our offices right," he once said. "We think it's important to have a high density of people. People are packed together everywhere. We all share offices."

April Fool's Joke?

When April Fool's Day 2004 rolled around, Larry and Sergey were ready in more ways than one. Playfully, the company's website announced the Google Copernicus Center, dubbed the Googlunaplex, a research facility to be opened on the moon. Striking a balance between high-tech jargon and silliness, the notice explained that Google would be studying "de-oxygenated cubicle dwelling," as well as "entropized information filtering, high-density, high delivery hosting." In case someone missed the joke, the latter phrase was abbreviated "HiDeHiDeHo."

That same day, Larry and Sergey issued a press release. This also had an amusing tone that may have fooled some people. It began with a statement that search is only the second most popular activity on the Internet, and the top one is e-mail. The announcement continued, "'Heck, Yeah,' Say Google Founders." It explained that Larry and Sergey had decided to offer a free e-mail service, dubbed Gmail, to selected users. They claimed their inspiration was a Google user who complained about the poor quality of her e-mail. "Can't you people fix this?" the press release quoted her.

IN FOCUS

Twenty Percent Time

Larry and Sergey believe that individual Googlers can make unique contributions to the company. To tap into their employees' creativity, they instituted a program called Twenty Percent Time. Googlers are encouraged to spend 20 percent of their work time (a full day out of a five-day week) working on any project they feel could lead to an innovative, useful service. "There is a feeling here of intellectual freedom," says Laszlo Beck, vice president of people operations.[9]

April 1, 2004

Google sets up e-mail—make that, Gmail

<u>From the Pages of</u>
<u>USA TODAY</u>

Internet search company Google today introduces a free Web-based e-mail program, Gmail, which it says solves the problem of finding information within e-mail letters and attachments.

"People have thousands of messages," says Google co-founder Sergey Brin. "Now, you can search through them for information anywhere you are, whether that's at home, in the office or in an Internet cafe."

Google, which is expected to go public later this year, is entering a field dominated by Microsoft and Yahoo. But Google offers substantially more storage space than other free Web e-mail programs. Microsoft and Yahoo give users 2 megabytes and 4 megabytes of space respectively, with constant reminders to delete files or upgrade to premium monthly subscription versions to get more storage.

Gmail offers 1 gigabyte of storage. Brin says Google can afford to do that because of the new kind of advertising it will bring to e-mail. Google will use its base of more than 150,000 advertisers to match their services with subjects in the e-mail. This is the same system that matches advertisers with search queries. For instance, an e-mail that discusses new car purchases might feature a text ad from a car dealer.

Gmail will start with a "soft launch," to 1,000 testers, Brin says. It will open up to the general public within the next three months. Users can start signing up at www.gmail.com.

Until now, much of the competitive attention on Google has focused on its search capabilities. The "search wars" heated up substantially since February, when Yahoo dumped Google in favor of its own new search technology. Microsoft said Friday it would unveil a search engine within the next 12 months.

Gmail is "Google saying, 'Look, you want to come after us in search, we'll come after you, as well,'" says Danny Sullivan, editor of *SearchEngineWatch* newsletter. "It puts the other guys on the defensive."

—Jefferson Graham

"If a Google user has a problem with e-mail, well, so do we," came Larry and Sergey's prompt response. Google proposed to fix the situation by providing users with a full gigabyte of memory to store their e-mails. This was more memory than any other company supplied. According to Google, people would be able to "hold onto their mail forever."

It sounded too good to be true. In fact, many people assumed it was simply another April Fool's joke. "It's going to go down in history as one of the biggest pranks ever pulled," wrote someone on the popular message poster Slashdot.org. Jonathan Rosenberg, Google's vice president of products, admitted, "We were having fun with this announcement." But he added, "We are very serious about Gmail."

Privacy Issue
There was more to Gmail than an almost unlimited capacity to store and retrieve e-mails. Although the service was free, Google planned to make money. It would include ads, or "sponsored links," with each Gmail. Special software would automatically scan each message to target which ads were appropriate to the content. For example, if someone wrote about a planned vacation, the person receiving the Gmail might notice sponsored links for airlines, travel agencies, or car rentals. Did this mean someone at Google was reading the Gmails? No, but many users were uneasy and indignant. They felt as if their privacy was being violated.

The resulting uproar surprised Larry and Sergey. "We're not keeping your mail or mining it or anything like that," Sergey stressed. "No one is looking. . . . Our ads aren't distracting. They're helpful." He also pointed out that other e-mail services routinely scanned messages to filter out spam (junk e-mail).

The controversy had the potential to harm Google's reputation and damage its business. But Larry and Sergey did not remove the ads. They believed that eventually all the fuss would die down and that the public would come to accept Gmail. Once again, their instincts proved to be correct.

www.usatoday.com

USA TODAY

Going public: Larry *(left)* and *Sergey (right)*, seen here at Google's headquarters in California in 2003, decided to take the company public in 2004.

"Not a Conventional Company"

On April 24, 2004, Larry and Sergey filed the official document declaring their intention to become a public company. It was not something they had planned to do. But certain federal regulations came into play. Because Google had made a great deal of money and given stock to many of its employees, the government required it to reveal its financial situation whether it remained private or went public. Offering public shares for sale would bring revenue to Google's employees and investors. Larry and Sergey felt that they owed it to these people to go public.

Both founders of Google knew that going public would change their lives. Used to doing things their own way, they worried about losing their privacy and freedom. When they weren't working, Larry and Sergey enjoyed outdoor activities and spending time with their girlfriends. They didn't want their freedom hampered by unwanted publicity. Professionally, they had misgivings too. They understood the business complications that can accompany a company's transition from private to public. Whatever happened, they were determined not to lose control of their company. Furthermore, they decided not to even follow the traditional rules for going public.

Larry and Sergey asserted their independence in the letter they submitted with their official registration statement. "Google is not a conventional company," they wrote. "We do not intend to become one. . . . We have managed Google differently. We have also emphasized an atmosphere of creativity and challenge." Larry and Sergey's letter made it clear that they were more interested in developing useful services and "improv[ing] the lives of as many people as possible" than they were in making huge profits. They were not afraid to take risks. "We aspire to make Google an institution that makes the world a better place," they declared.

A Different Kind of IPO

When most private businesses go public, they turn the process over to investment bankers, who set the price of the stock that will be sold. Often small investors receive little opportunity to buy stock. The investment firms decide who will have a chance to purchase most of the shares. Larry and Sergey thought this system was unfair. They chose to offer their stock through a different process that gave everyone a chance to participate in the IPO. The price of their stock was set through an auction rather than determined by investment bankers.

Everyone who owns stock in a company has a small say in the way that company is run. This system posed a challenge to Larry and Sergey. Could they be outvoted by their own stockholders? To prevent that from happening, they decided to have two classes of stockholders. Regular investors would receive Class A stock, which gave them one vote for each share. Larry and Sergey, however, would hold Class B stock, which gave them ten votes per share. They would continue to make all the important decisions concerning Google's future. Some people questioned the fairness of such a division. "Google wants to have its cake and eat it too," complained one business owner. But Larry and Sergey felt their unusual system was best for the company. They knew better than anyone else how to run Google.

An Interview with *Playboy*

Larry and Sergey rarely gave interviews. But the same month they filed to go public, they made an exception. They agreed to talk to a reporter for *Playboy* magazine. When David Sheff, a contributing editor from the magazine, arrived at the Googleplex, Sergey was playing a vigorous game of volleyball. Sheff noted that Sergey had to be "dragged in shoeless from the court." Full of restless energy, Larry and Sergey remained on their feet as they fielded the reporter's questions. Sheff wrote that "they leaned on their chair backs,

Getting the scoop: Sergey and Larry agreed to be interviewed for *Playboy* magazine by writer David Sheff *(above)* in 2004, before the company went public.

climbed on their chairs and wandered about the windowed conference room. It's apparently impossible to sit still when you're engaged in changing the world." From Google's phone system to the company motto, privacy, and censorship issues, Larry and Sergey made a thorough and accurate representation of their company. Knowing that more than ten billion websites existed, Sheff asked, "Is it possible for Google to keep up?"

"We have to," replied Larry.

Sergey went a step further. "Ultimately you want to have the entire world's knowledge connected directly to your mind. . . . We probably won't be looking up everything on a computer." He envisioned a future in which we can have "the entirety of the world's information as just one of our thoughts." On that incredible note, Sheff ended his magazine piece.

The Public Reacts

Many people felt that Sergey and Larry picked the wrong time to talk to *Playboy*. The last few weeks before a business goes public are known as a "quiet period." Company officials are not supposed to talk about their company or say anything that might affect the price of its stock. But Larry and Sergey had reasoned the story about them would not appear in *Playboy* until September—after their IPO was over.

As it turned out, Larry and Sergey were wrong. The September issue of the magazine came out in August. This meant people got to read their comments before their company went public. Some observers felt that Google's entry into the stock exchange should be postponed. It looked as if Larry and Sergey had destroyed their own IPO. After all their preparations, however, Larry and Sergey were not to be put off. They simply added their interview to the official documents. By doing this, they ensured they had not revealed to the public information they had withheld in their application. In this way, they got around their technical violation of the quiet period.

Despite mistakes, unfavorable publicity, and last-minute price changes, Google achieved a spectacularly successful IPO. On August 19, 2004, Larry rang the opening bell at the NASDAQ exchange. Although Google sold only a small amount of its stock, the company made $1.6 billion. The price for one share jumped from $85 to $100 in the course of a single day. Employees who owned stock became rich overnight. By November the price had doubled to $200 per share. Later, CEO Eric Schmidt compared the much-criticized IPO to a "turbulent [airplane] flight." He felt satisfied that Google had made a safe and happy landing.

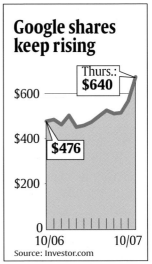

Google shares keep rising

Thurs.: **$640**

$600

$400 **$476**

$200

0
10/06   10/07

Source: Investor.com

By Adrienne Lewis, USA TODAY, 2007

Pushing Forward

A landing implies that the journey is over. But in many ways, Google was poised to take off. In October 2004, the company opened new offices in Ireland and India. Larry and Sergey turned up in these sites to launch the new facilities with fanfare. That December a new research and development center opened in Tokyo, Japan. Google was spreading out in exciting new ways. February 2005 saw the launch of Google Maps. Users looking for a particular site could use a mouse to extend the street map in any direction. Just three months later, the company introduced Google Earth, which combined satellite images and maps with fantastic results. The proper software allowed a person to make a virtual visit to anyplace on Earth, zooming in for close-up views.

Every month Google achieved major milestones with new offices or services. Larry and Sergey also purchased smaller companies with promising new technology. As their own company grew, they no longer knew everyone by name. But they held weekly meetings, or TGIFs

Emergency Role for Google Earth

In September 2005, a terrible hurricane, Katrina, struck New Orleans, Louisiana, and the Gulf of Mexico coast. Relying on Google Earth for vital information, the Coast Guard compared views of the area before and after the devastation. This approach allowed rescue workers to pinpoint the locations of the worst flooding and to find people stranded on rooftops. Not long after Hurricane Katrina, a powerful earthquake rocked Pakistan. Once again, Google Earth provided valuable information on road conditions and on the state of isolated villages. Although the imagery was not as detailed as workers would have liked, it significantly aided rescue efforts. Cooperating with several other organizations, including the United Nations, Google provided vital service after another powerful earthquake devastated Haiti in January 2010. Rescue workers relied on Google Earth to keep track of refugee sites and tent camps. Jean-Philippe Chauzy, a representative for the Inter-

Helping in Haiti: This Google Earth map of Port-au-Prince, Haiti, allowed officials to chart population density movements after the earthquake in that country in 2010.

national Organization for Migration, said, "It is the first time a tool of such sophistication has been deployed in such short order by humanitarian actors after a major emergency."

(Thank Goodness It's Friday), in which employees were encouraged to express concerns and share ideas. Music and food featured prominently in these sessions. New Googlers (Nooglers) stood out in their

Vint Cerf

Computer engineer Vint Cerf joined Google in 2005. Larry and Sergey were delighted to welcome a Googler who is often hailed as the father of the Internet. In 1974 Cerf had written a set of rules for sending information between computers. They were called transmission control protocol, or TCP. Before TCP, there was no consensus on rules for sharing documents between computers. Differing protocols meant that many computers could not communicate with one another. Cerf's contribution paved the way for the Internet as we know it. At Google, Cerf focuses on the future as he investigates the ways in which the World Wide Web is changing society.

Father of the Internet: Sergey and Larry hired renowned computer engineer Vint Cerf *(above)* in 2005.

special beanies topped with propellers. By then in their early thirties, Larry and Sergey complemented each other as they led the proceedings. According to author Ken Auletta, Sergey is "funnier and tends to dominate." But Larry doesn't mind. He enjoys Sergey's humor as much as anyone.

In the eight years since Google's founding, the World Wide Web had exploded beyond most people's imagination. Not only had the number of Web pages soared, but audio and video clips were also appearing at a fantastic rate. Larry and Sergey wanted to keep pace with the astronomical expansion. In October 2006, they purchased the Internet video service YouTube for $1.6 billion. With its emphasis on "entertainment and social networking," YouTube seemed a somewhat unusual acquisition for a company focused on information. Sergey Brin explained, "When I perform a search, I often find that the best answer

IN FOCUS

Challenged in Court

In its brief history, Google has faced a number of lawsuits. In October 2005, the Authors Guild and the Association of American Publishers filed a suit. They charged that Google's project to digitize all the world's books and put short portions online violated the rights of both authors and publishers. Three years later, the parties reached a settlement in which Google agreed to compensate those whose copyrights had been violated as well as to pay legal fees and to set up a Books Rights Registry. In return, the company could proceed with its digitizing project.

Sergey hailed the agreement as a "win-win" situation. He insisted that "the real victors [were] the readers. The tremendous wealth of knowledge that lies within the books of the world will be at their fingertips."

But the $125 million settlement to the lawsuit was not the end of the story. The U.S. Department of Justice raised concerns about the project, now called Google Books, that had to be addressed in court. These include privacy and copyright issues, as well as the huge advantage the settlement gives Google over other companies. James Grimmelmann, a professor at New York Law School and a former computer programmer, considers the debate "the most important copyright dispute we're currently facing. I would say this whole controversy has the potential to really affect how we access all kinds of media, not just old ones, but also new ones." As of June 2010, the results of the Justice Department's case against Google are still pending.

www.usatoday.com

USA TODAY

Money

SECTION B

December 20, 2004

Google units include social networking, photos, maps

From the Pages of
USA TODAY

MOUNTAIN VIEW, Calif.—In Google-land, search is no longer just about locating Internet Web pages.

The 2005 mantra for the world's most popular search engine is "bringing more information you want."

"One of the important issues with search is, if we don't have it in our index, we can't return an answer," says Google co-founder Sergey Brin.

Putting more information into its mammoth index was the impetus for Google's recent groundbreaking deal to digitize five huge library collections, including the New York Public Library, Stanford and Oxford. Many of the books should be scanned and available for reading online by early next year.

But Google's expansion plans go way beyond dusting off old books and making them available to the masses. In the past few months, Google has added several offerings that seemingly have nothing to do with search, including:

- Social networking site Orkut. Named after Google engineer Orkut Buyukkokten, it's a place where potential business associates, friends and singles can linger and discuss topics of interest.
- Photo organization software Picasa. Users paid $29 for Picasa before Google bought the company from Idealab earlier this year for an undisclosed sum. Now, the software, which helps find and edit digital photographs, is free. A

is not necessarily a Web page. I know that sounds like heresy coming from Google, but in fact, if you are learning a sport, if you want to build a house, if you want to study a science, often videos are the best medium to learn about those things, to learn how to do those things."

new, greatly enhanced—and still free—version of Picasa will be released in January.

- Maps. Google's Keyhole takes Internet map location to a new level. Instead of looking up someone's address, this program takes a 3-D aerial view of the neighborhood. It can zoom in to show a specific block, with amazing precision.

No mere portal

With all these digital tools—plus a popular e-mail program and links to news sites—don't tell executives here at the "Googleplex" in Silicon Valley that Google is becoming a Web portal, like Yahoo and MSN.

For years, Google has said its focus was simply on search. Executives, often in language that can only be described as Google-speak, insist it still is.

"We want to be what the user wants, when he or she wants it, as opposed to everything the user might want, even if they don't," says Marissa Mayer, Google's director of consumer products.

Searching for files, photos

Perhaps Google's most acclaimed innovation of the year was the October launch of software that hunts for files on a computer's hard drive. Competitors had to scramble to catch up. Microsoft and Ask Jeeves introduced desk-top search programs last week, and Yahoo says it will have one in January.

Desk-top search is another way for Google to keep users loyal for more hours a day. The same theory applies to Google's entry into free digital-photo software.

How Google will make money giving away software that used to cost $30 "is the number one question I get," says Picasa general manager Lars Perkins.

Digital photography is so popular, "Google wants to be in the middle of how we manage this kind of content," Perkins says. "We'll figure out how to monetize it later."

With more than $2 billion in advertising revenue so far this year, they might just do that.

—Jefferson Graham

Censorship in China

All over the world, people turned to Google. But sometimes foreign laws interfered with the search engine's objectivity. Since 2002 Google had been operating an edition of its search engine in the Chinese

October 18, 2005

Google Print project inspires fans, fears

<u>From the Pages of</u>
<u>USA TODAY</u>

LOS ANGELES—For a recent comparative literature class paper, Brendan Draper wanted to quote a phrase from a novel he'd read, but he couldn't remember what page it was on.

He typed "nervous condition" into Internet search giant Google's index of books. Within seconds, he found the phrase and page number of the book. "It was extremely helpful," says Draper, 20, a student at the West Chester University of Pennsylvania.

Situations like his are exactly what Google had in mind a year ago when it unveiled the Google Print project at the Frankfurt Book Fair in Germany. Google co-founders Larry Page and Sergey Brin, on hand for the event, told publishers they wanted to scan their books, at no cost, to make them searchable online and to help sell copies to consumers.

Google returns to the fair Tuesday to tout the program—and to announce searches in French, Spanish, Italian and German. But it is no longer reaping the initial positive glow from publishers. Instead, it finds itself in the position of having to defend itself to the industry.

language. Two years later, Google News came to China. The Chinese government did not want its citizens exposed to some of the political views available in various online publications and wanted Google to censor its search results. Its refusal to do so angered government officials. They frequently blocked Google altogether within China and its territories.

Larry and Sergey faced a soul-searching dilemma. For months they

How it works

The Google Print homepage—www.print.google.com—lets users search for a phrase, character or other term to turn up a link to a related book title. Clicking on the book title generates an image of the page of the book, along with other information about it and advertising links to online bookstores. Google splits the revenue from those ads with publishers.

The entire contents of public domain books are available for viewing; for books under copyright, just a few pages or in some cases, only bibliographic data and brief snippets.

Content in Google Print comes from two sources: publishers and libraries. Google infuriated publishers after it announced an alliance last December with five libraries, including Harvard and the University of Michigan, to scan their entire collections. Google said its objective was to build the world's largest online card catalog.

Some critics in the book industry fear the library program will spark the kind of piracy problems that have beset the music and film industries. To appease publishers, Google suspended plans to scan copyrighted books until Nov. 1, although it is still scanning books at the request of copyright holders.

"Google is taking our property and not paying for it. It's burglary," says Nick Taylor, president of the Authors Guild, a New York-based association that has filed a copyright infringement suit against Google. The suit is supported by the Association of American Publishers.

Google Print product manager Adam Smith says the biggest misconception is that Google's master plan is to display entire books online. "We don't have permission to do that," he says. "We're a finding tool, like a digital card catalog."

Google associate general counsel Nicole Wong says that because Google puts only small portions of copyrighted books online, it has fair use rights. "We are not trying to republish their book," she says.

—Jefferson Graham

discussed the pros and cons. "We actually did an evil scale," said Eric Schmidt. If they continued to defy censorship, the Chinese people would have no access to any Google search results. If they agreed to remove certain political sites from the search results, Chinese citizens could at least view other materials.

Larry and Sergey decided the second choice was the lesser of two evils. In October 2006, they launched Google.cn, a separate website in China. Google alerted Chinese users when it blocked results. It also refused to gather personal information on Chinese users that the government might be able to use against these individuals. But people all over the world criticized Google for giving in to the Chinese censors. Sergey himself later admitted that the company

IN FOCUS

Showdown in China

In January 2010, Google announced that it had been the victim of cyber-attacks originating in China. Although Google has faced other such attacks, this one was particularly alarming. Investigations suggested that the perpetrators had accessed the Gmail accounts of Chinese citizens and people of other nationalities who champion human rights in China. Outraged Google officials declared they would no longer submit to Chinese censorship, even if the company had to withdraw from China. But Google hoped to find a solution to the dilemma that would allow it to continue operating in the country. "Our focus has really been what's best for the Chinese people," Sergey Brin told the *Los Angeles Times*. "It's not been about our revenue and profit."

When negotiations failed to produce an agreement, Google made good on its promise to stop censoring its results and its news service, a move the *Wall Street Journal* described as a "risky and dramatic act of defiance." The company began rerouting visitors from its Chinese website to another Google site in Hong Kong that remains uncensored. In an interview with the *Wall Street Journal*, Sergey explained that developments in China had brought back unpleasant memories of his early childhood in Russia, especially visits to his home by the Soviet police and the discrimination his father faced as a Jew.

"I think at some point it is appropriate to stand up for your principles," he said, "and if more companies, governments, individuals did that, I do think the world would be a better place."

IN FOCUS

VIP Visitors

Google attracts some high-profile visitors to its Mountain View headquarters, including former vice president Al Gore, who is a staunch supporter of the Internet, and all the candidates in the U.S. presidential election of 2008. President Barack Obama, who is also a fan of Google, feels he has something in common with Larry Page, Sergey Brin, and Eric Schmidt. "What we shared," he said, describing a 2007 visit, "is a belief in changing the world from the bottom up not from the top down."

Obama at Google: Barack Obama *(left)*, then running for president, talks with Google CEO Eric Schmidt *(right)* at the Google offices in 2007.

had "compromised" its ethical standards. The decision had been especially hard for him because his parents had suffered under a restrictive government in the Soviet Union. But he and Larry hoped that Google's presence in China, even censored, provided some good to the people of that nation.

Hybrid Philanthropy

Two years after their IPO, Larry and Sergey had not forgotten their goal "to make Google an institution that makes the world a better place." In 2006 they hired Larry Brilliant as the first director of Google's philanthropic (charitable) activities. World health and developing renewable, environmentally friendly forms of energy became top priorities for the company.

A company like Google could improve lives in two ways. It could donate money to important causes, and it could develop new technologies for helping solve pressing problems. Google combined both methods in a concept called hybrid philanthropy. Simply put, Google contributed funds to other organizations and looked for ways to help on its own. In keeping with its humanitarian mission, Google scientists investigated the causes and possible long-term consequence of climate change,

Brilliant philanthropy: Larry Brilliant, shown here in 2008, was hired as Google's first director of philanthropy in 2006. He had previously been a CEO of two companies and worked with the World Health Organization in the campaign to rid the world of smallpox.

or global warming. They studied nonpolluting energy sources that are cleaner than coal, such as wind power and geothermal energy. Larry, Sergey, and Larry Brilliant took a step in the direction of safe, clean energy when they had more than nine thousand solar panels installed at the Googleplex in May 2007. These large flat panels, situated on the roof, take sunlight and turn it into energy needed to keep the facilities running.

"But just providing energy for Google is not enough of a goal," Larry Page said. Heedless once again of what seems "impossible," he had a

Googleplex panels: This aerial view of the Google headquarters in California shows the solar panels on the roofs of many of the buildings.

specific goal in mind. He wanted to build a clean-energy power plant big enough to supply all the needs of a city as large as San Francisco. As Larry Brilliant explained, "We do lots of hardware stuff at Google. This company, because of its success, touches on every controversial aspect of life."

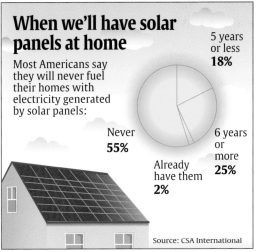

USA TODAY Snapshots®

When we'll have solar panels at home

Most Americans say they will never fuel their homes with electricity generated by solar panels:

5 years or less
18%

Never
55%

6 years or more
25%

Already have them
2%

Source: CSA International

By Anne R. Carey and Veronica Salazar, USA TODAY, 2009

USA TODAY

Money

SECTION B

November 28, 2007

Google to seek cheaper, cleaner energy sources

From the Pages of
USA TODAY

Internet giant Google is expanding from search and advertising to try developing cheap energy alternatives to coal.

The initiative, Renewable Energy Cheaper than Coal, will focus initially on solar, geothermal and wind energy.

Google will use its vast resources to buy companies and hire engineers to see this initiative through. "Our goal is to produce one gigawatt of renewable energy capacity that is cheaper than coal," Google co-founder Larry Page said Tuesday. "We are optimistic this can be done in years, not decades."

One gigawatt can power a city the size of San Francisco, with 750,000 residents, Google says.

Google got interested in helping fund new renewable energy sources because it is a huge consumer of electricity for its big data centers. They house hundreds of thousands of computers that run the Google search engine. Additionally, it wants to help solve the global warming crisis, and says cheaper and cleaner energy sources can help do that.

Piper Jaffray analyst Gene Munster expects Google to spend $500 million on the project, or 3% of its cash holdings.

Co-founder Sergey Brin says expanding into energy doesn't take away from Google's goal of organizing the world's information. The company works on what it calls the 70/20/10 rule. That is, 70% of its efforts go to the core businesses of search and advertising, 20% to adjacent areas and 10% to anything Google engineers feel like pursuing.

Renewable energy experts welcomed Google's entry. "Google sells a product you can't put your hands on that people love to use, which isn't dissimilar from the electric utility business," says Mike Eckhart, president of the American Council on Renewable Energy.

Google will "attract very good people," says Steve Chu, director of the University of California's Lawrence Berkeley National Laboratory.

Brin was asked on a conference call with reporters how Google could preach for new energy while executives crisscross the globe on its company jets. "To deal with climate change, you have to tackle the big problems," he said. "To think that people are going to stop traveling is unrealistic."

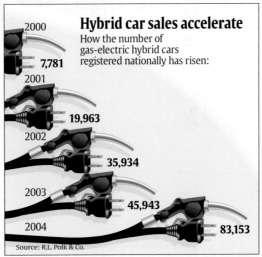

USA TODAY Snapshots®

Hybrid car sales accelerate
How the number of gas-electric hybrid cars registered nationally has risen:

2000 7,781
2001 19,963
2002 35,934
2003 45,943
2004 83,153

Source: R.L. Polk & Co.

By Mark Pearson and Marcy E. Mullins, USA TODAY, 2005

Google watchers are "skeptical" about the latest move, says analyst Greg Sterling of Sterling Market Intelligence. "They seem to be getting into so many areas outside of search. There's a quality to this aspiration that's a little hard to accept, because it's so ambitious."

In the last year, Google announced moves outside of search, including an attempt to develop an open operating system for cellphones based on Google technology, and buying wireless spectrum for a cellphone network.

"If we look ahead to Google in five years, it will be primarily a search company," Munster says. "Their core business will be unchanged."

—Jefferson Graham

Diverse interests: Sergey *(left)* and Larry *(right)* tackled many different issues through Google. Here, in 2008, they explain a feature of Google Maps that allows users to be given a choice of public transportation options, in addition to driving directions.

Optimistic Future

Larry's and Sergey's responsibilities pulled them in many directions. Luckily, their girlfriends shared their deep commitment to education, health care, and environmental issues as well as their interest in technology.

Sergey and Anne

Sergey had been dating Anne Wojcicki. The two met through Anne's sister Susan, who had rented Larry and Sergey their first off-campus office space in her garage. A graduate of Yale University, Anne worked in health care as an investment analyst. Like Sergey, she enjoyed athletics. In college she ice-skated and participated in varsity ice hockey.

When Anne and Sergey decided to get married in 2007, they opted for an unusual ceremony. Secrecy surrounded every phase of their planning. According to reports, the guests themselves did not know where the wedding was to take place—even as they boarded Larry and Sergey's private jet. The plane took the guests to an island in the Bahamas. Then they swam or were ferried to a nearby sandbar. Anne, in a white swimsuit, and Sergey, in black, swam to the site where they exchanged vows under a traditional Jewish wedding canopy. It's said that Sergey also followed the old Jewish custom of smashing a wineglass.

Lots in common: Sergey and Anne Wojcicki *(right)* met through Anne's sister Susan, who had rented Sergey and Larry their first office space—her garage. Sergey and Anne are shown here in New York City in 2008.

Larry and Lucinda

About six months later, in November, the *San Francisco Chronicle* announced, "Now the other Google founder is planning a secret wedding." Larry Page and his girlfriend, Lucinda (Lucy) Southworth, had been dating for over a year. A former model and a doctoral student at Stanford, she had degrees from the University of Pennsylvania and Oxford University. She had also gone to South Africa to do medical work and shared Larry's desire to "better the world."

Like Sergey and Anne, Larry and Lucy flew their guests to an island for the ceremony. On December 8, 2007, six hundred people from all over the world watched Larry and Lucy exchange vows on Necker Island, a privately owned property in the Caribbean.

Active Lifestyle

As jammed as their schedules were, Larry and Sergey made time for recreation too. They took up the relatively new sport of kite surfing, also called kiteboarding. Summers, they joined other enthusiasts, many of them engineers, at a popular beach near Mountain View. As they balanced on surfboards, kites that resemble parachutes pulled them across the water. Craving even further excitement, Larry trained to become a helicopter pilot and Sergey built a sailboat that will be powered by a kite. Both men also liked to travel and take photographs.

Sergey likes to kiteboard so much, he even considered doing it on a business trip to Israel. Interviewing Sergey for Ha-aretz, the Israeli news service, reporter Guy Rolnik remarked lightly, "So you prefer kiteboarding to finishing your doctorate." Sergey chuckled as he replied, "I might pick up inspiration for my PhD. while kiteboarding."

All "Grown Up"

Just before Google's annual general meeting in May 2008, Eric Schmidt humorously informed reporters, "The boys have grown up." But he also said that their clothing hasn't changed at all. Instead of the usual coat and tie, Larry and Sergey, aged thirty-five and thirty-four, respectively, came to the meeting in casual pullover shirts. "They care a lot about the principles of the company," Eric said. "They don't care a lot about the other things." Hadn't their status as billionaires changed their lives? reporters wanted to know. "I do have a pretty good toy budget now," admitted Sergey. "I just got a new [computer] monitor." Larry replied even more simply, "I don't have to do laundry."

For Sergey the ultimate adventure may prove to be space travel. In June 2007, he paid five million dollars for a possible seat on a future trip to the International Space Station. A Virginia company called Space Adventures was selling the seats in a Russian Soyuz spacecraft. "I am a big believer in the exploration and commercial development of the space frontier," Sergey said. His chance to fly may come in 2011 or 2012.

Google in Space

In early September 2008, Sergey and Anne and Larry and Lucy watched with excitement as a satellite launched from Vandenberg Air Force Base near Santa Barbara, California. Thanks to a special deal with Geoeye satellite imaging company, the craft heading for orbit was the first to bear the brightly colored Google logo. When it achieved orbit at an altitude of 423 miles (680 km), it would circle Earth more than a dozen times each day. Google would use photos and information from the satellite to provide better resolution and more detailed pictures for its Google Maps and Google Earth services.

September 14, 2007

Google offers $20M as moon rover prize

From the Pages of
USA TODAY
Nearly 40 years after the U.S. beat the Soviets to the moon, Internet giant Google said Thursday it will give $20 million to the first private group to land a roving robot on the lunar surface.

The purse is being offered by the X Prize Foundation, which awarded $10 million in 2005 to a group that included Microsoft co-founder Paul Allen for launching a human into space.

In the '70s, the Soviets launched the only robotic rovers to have negotiated the moon. Budget woes forced NASA this spring to cancel its lunar-rover plan.

Google is taking part because the contest "is really going to accomplish something very, very impressive," company co-founder Sergey Brin said Thursday in a video announcement. The goal is "something . . . only a couple of governments have ever accomplished." . . .

National Aeronautics and Space Administration (NASA) plans to send astronauts back to the moon by 2020 and establish a lunar research camp, but Peter Worden of NASA said the contest doesn't threaten the agency. Such private space exploration "is exactly what we hoped would happen," he said. "NASA is pretty excited about this."

Peter Diamandis, X Prize chairman, said he expects entrants from the USA, China, Europe and Japan and hopes the first flight will launch in 2010 or 2011.

—Traci Watson

The next year, the world celebrated the fortieth anniversary of the first Apollo moon landing. Google was ready with a different kind of launch—the debut of Moon in Google Earth. The new application did not use satellite imagery, but it did allow viewers to see close-up views of landing sites and TV coverage of the Apollo flights. Google also celebrated space achievements through the Google Lunar X-Prize.

Announced in 2007, the prize will award $20 million to the first private company that lands a robot on the moon and sends back a gigabyte of images.

Another Kind of Challenge

It seemed that Larry and Sergey had everything young men could want—success, adventure, and happy personal lives. But a shadow lay over Sergey. Before his marriage, he had learned that his mother has Parkinson's disease. A neurological disorder, Parkinson's is characterized by tremors, shakiness, and slurred speech. In the course of investigating the disease, Sergey and Anne visited Linda Avey, who was conducting research on genetic factors related to Parkinson's.

Anne shared Linda's keen interest in genetics. Eventually the two became partners in founding a new company, 23andMe. Twenty-three refers to the number of chromosome pairs each person possesses. Chromosomes contain the genes that determine most characteristics of living things. Linda and Anne's company would give clients a chance to learn their personal genetic background by submitting a sample of their DNA (unique combination of genes that determines a person's characteristics). Among other things, such information can let a person know if he or she has a predisposition to certain diseases, such as Parkinson's.

Although he usually guards his privacy, Sergey decided to share the results of his genetic profile at a Google conference in 2008. He announced that he carries a rare mutation that increases his risk of developing Parkinson's disease. "I feel fortunate to be in this position," he wrote in a personal blog. "Until the fountain of youth is discovered, all of us will have some conditions in our old age, only we don't know what they will be. I have a better guess than almost anyone else what ills may be mine—and I have decades to prepare for it."

Sergey's genetic results came at an especially crucial time. In December Anne gave birth to the couple's first child, a little boy named Benji. Parenthood gave Sergey one more reason to fight for a cure.

In March 2009, Sergey announced that Google would donate huge sums of money for a study of the disease to be done by 23andMe. Patients with Parkinson's could sign up for the study online. By studying their DNA and comparing it with the DNA of people without Parkinson's, scientists might be able to identify other genetic factors related to the disorder. Sergey has volunteered his own DNA to the study. Ever the pragmatist, he has told reporters, "I kind of give myself 50-50 odds of getting Parkinson's in 20 or so years, 25 years. But I also give it a 50-50 shot of medicine catching up to be able to deal with it." Meanwhile, Sergey continues to support research to improve the odds for himself and others living with the risk of Parkinson's.

Cloud Computing

Larry, Sergey, and others at Google and elsewhere believe that the future belongs to the Internet in ways that are just beginning to develop. For many years, most software, such as word processing programs, has been located directly in individuals' personal computers. But new versions of such standard software appear constantly. Sometimes these newer versions don't work well on older computers. Larry and Sergey foresee a different model. Instead of standard applications and services being located in personal computers, they will be located on the Internet. People will not be limited to their own computers. They will be able to access whatever services they need from any computer they use. They will also be able to store their personal documents on the Internet.

In some technical drawings, the Internet is represented by a cloud. For this reason, the new model of Internet service is known as cloud computing. Sometimes it is also called software as a service.

Sergey and Larry became proud parents within one year of each other. In November 2009, Larry's son was born.

Internet Freedom v. Privacy

Google has faced many lawsuits. One case concerned a video in which a disabled boy was taunted by his classmates in Torino, Italy. Posted on Google in 2006, the clip provoked angry protests. Eventually Google officials in Italy removed the video, but three Google executives were tried in Italy for violation of that country's privacy laws. The prosecution argued that the offending video should have been removed instantly instead of running for almost two months. In February 2010, the defendants were convicted and given six-month suspended sentences. "We are very satisfied," said the prosecutors. "Because by means of this trial we have posed a serious problem: that is to say, the protection of human beings, which must prevail over corporate interests."

Disagreeing vigorously, Google issued a statement calling the outcome an "astonishing decision ... that attacks the very principles of freedom on which the Internet is built. Common sense dictates that only the person who films and uploads a video to a hosting platform [such as Google] could take the steps necessary to protect the privacy and obtain the consent of the people they are filming."

What's Next?

By 2007 Google offered about 150 products to the public. It was branching out in advertising and in applications that could be used on mobile phones. It was working to develop high-speed cloud computing. The company's offices were located all over the world. "And what's next for Google?" The question pops up at the end of the milestones listed on Google's website. But the answer is vague. "We don't talk much about what lies ahead," concludes the list of Google's accomplishments, "because we believe one of our chief competitive advantages is surprise."

www.usatoday.com

USA TODAY

Money

SECTION B

February 11, 2010

Google plans to test superfast Internet

From the Pages of
USA TODAY

Google on Wednesday vowed to build and test a rocket-fast Internet service to as many as 500,000 people, positioning the search giant as a potential rival to cable and phone companies.

Google said it intends to build in a few trial communities a fiber-optic network that can transmit 1 gigabit of data per second—fast enough to deliver a high-definition movie in five minutes. Typical cable and phone broadband services transmit 5 megabits per second, which can mean hours for such a download.

"We don't think we have all the answers—but through our trial, we hope to make a meaningful contribution to the shared goal of delivering faster and better Internet for everyone," the company said in an announcement on its blog. It says it wants software developers to come up with applications, including "uses we can't yet imagine."

Google didn't say how much it would invest. It asked local officials to apply before March 26 to have the network in their communities.

The company says it will allow other Internet providers to use its system. Advocates of network neutrality—where providers treat all websites equally—said the test could prove it's possible to profit from a competitively priced service on an open system.

"Big broadband creates big opportunities," Federal Communications Commission Chairman Julius Genachowski said. "This significant trial will provide an American test bed for the next generation of innovative, high-speed Internet apps, devices and services."

Andrew Schwartzman, CEO of the Media Access Project, a public interest law firm, says Google's plan could encourage "other providers to recognize the value of opening their networks."

—David Lieberman, with Edward C. Baig and Byron Acohido

Larry Page gave a hint of the far future, however, when he said, "Artificial intelligence would be the ultimate version of Google.... It would understand exactly what you wanted, and it would give you the right thing. That's obviously artificial intelligence, to be able to answer any question, basically, because almost everything is on the Web, right? We're nowhere near doing that now. However, we can get ... closer to that, and that is basically what we're working on."

Perhaps Larry and Sergey's philosophy can best be summed up in a popular company saying, "More data is better data." The more you know about a topic or a problem, the better decisions you will be able to make. One of Sergey's favorite stories illustrates the point. Before Google was even three years old,

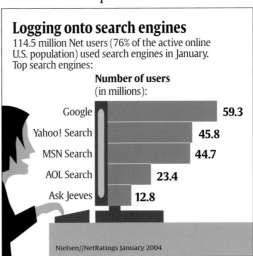

USA TODAY Snapshots®

Logging onto search engines
114.5 million Net users (76% of the active online U.S. population) used search engines in January. Top search engines:

Number of users (in millions):

Search engine	Users
Google	59.3
Yahoo! Search	45.8
MSN Search	44.7
AOL Search	23.4
Ask Jeeves	12.8

Nielsen//NetRatings January 2004

By Shannon Reilly and Sam Ward, USA TODAY, 2004

old, he received a letter from a man who turned to Google at a crisis moment. Feeling an unfamiliar pressure in his chest, the man sought information on heart disease. A list of results, beginning with information from the American Heart Association, appeared in less than a tenth of a second. The man concluded that he was having a heart attack and hurried to the hospital, where immediate surgery saved his life. "People really care about their information," said Sergey in an interview. "It's their career, it's their health, it's their education."

www.usatoday.com

USA TODAY

News

SECTION A

January 6, 2010

Google launches its own smartphone to take on Apple

<u>From the Pages of USA TODAY</u>

Taking direct aim at Apple's iPhone, Google on Tuesday introduced its most advanced phone to date the Nexus One and opened an online store to sell it directly to consumers.

The phone, available at google.com/phone, costs $179 with a two-year contract from T-Mobile. Similar offers will be available from Verizon Wireless and British carrier Vodafone this year.

You can buy the phone without a contract for $529.

The Nexus One runs an updated version of Google's Android operating system. Built by HTC from Google's direct specifications, it has a touch-screen and a fast processor. It includes a 5-megapixel camera for video and photos, a Global Positioning System (GPS), and stereo Bluetooth connection for headphones.

Among gee-whiz features: speech dictation, which lets you speak and compose e-mail messages, Twitter tweets and Facebook posts without typing.

Google has lagged Apple in the mobile market. It has tried to be a major player with Android, which it offers free to manufacturers and wireless carriers. Some 20 Android phones are available, but few, with the exception of the Verizon Droid (by Motorola), have been big sellers.

The Nexus One could change that, says Charles Golvin, an analyst at Forrester Research: "It's the best Android to date."

—Jefferson Graham

And it may get even easier to find crucial facts in the future. Larry foresees a time when people may simply carry a small computer with them at all times—much the way people carry cell phones. But his confidence extends way beyond the future of information technology.

Google in the future: Larry *(left)* and Sergey *(right)* believe that Google can make people's lives better.

"Look at the things that drive people's basic level of happiness," he said, "safety and opportunity for their kids, plus basic things like health and shelter. I think our ability to achieve these things on a large scale for many people in the world is improving."

That is how Larry and Sergey view Google's role—making life better for everyone. Through Google's rapidly multiplying services and efforts to save the environment, improve health care, and bring technological progress to underdeveloped nations, Larry and Sergey are doing their part to transform the world. The future is wide open.

GLOSSARY

AdSense: an advertising program that enables websites to make money by allowing ads to be posted

AdWords: Google's first advertising model in which clearly marked ads are placed beside relevant search results

algorithm: a set of complicated equations that allows Google to analyze the links on the World Wide Web and to index the Web

backlink: a link into a website from another site

browser: software that allows a computer to access the World Wide Web

client computer: a computer that provides access to the World Wide Web but does not store Web pages

cloud computing: a model for computing in which services and applications are stored directly on the Internet rather than on personal computers

crawler: a computer program that visits websites and identifies the links between them. Also called a spider or a robot.

domain name: a website's unique address

hypertext transfer protocol (http): a set of procedures that allows one computer to transfer information to another computer

Internet: a "network of networks" that allows computers to communicate with one another

link: an Internet connection between two documents or Web pages

search engine: a computer program that scans the World Wide Web to provide results for clients' search queries

server computer: a computer that stores, or holds the codes for, Web pages

server farm: warehouse where many server computers are stacked in tall towers

Silicon Valley: an area south of San Francisco, California, where thousands of computer and electronics companies are located

uniform resource locator (url): a unique address assigned to every Web document

World Wide Web: a body of interconnected documents and Web pages that are accessible through the Internet

SOURCE NOTES

5   Steven Levy and Brad Stone, "A Very Public Offering: After Months of Anticipation, the Sultans of Search Have Finally Announced Their IOP. And They're Doing It Their Own Way. (Google Inc.'s Initial Public Offering)," *Newsweek*, May 10, 2004, http://www.highbeam.com/doc/1G1-116191462.html (October 1, 2009).

6   Larry Page and Sergey Brin, "2004 Founders' IPO Letter, from the S-1 Registration Statement; 'An Owner's Manual' for Google's Shareholders," Google, 2009, http://investor.google.com/corporate/2004/ipo-founders-letter.html (June 11, 2010).

9   David A. Vise and Mark Malseed, *The Google Story*, updated edition (New York: Dell Trade Paperbacks, 2008), 24.

9   Larry Page, "Larry Page's University of Michigan Commencement Address," Google Press Center, May 2, 2009, http://www.google.com/intl/en/press/annc/20090502-page-commencement.html (May 6, 2009).

9   Ibid.

10 Vise and Malseed, 24.

10 American Academy of Achievement, "Larry Page Interview," Academy of Achievement, October 28, 2000, http://www.achievement/org/autodoc/page/pag0int-1 (May 4, 2009).

10 Richard L. Brandt, *Inside Larry and Sergey's Brain* (New York: Portfolio, 2009), 23.

10 American Academy of Achievement.

11 "Larry Page and Sergey Brin, "Founders of Google.com Credit Their Montessori Education for Much of Their Success on Prime-Time Television," IMC-Enews, 2004, http://www.montessori.org/enews/barbara_walters.html (September 1, 2009).

12 American Academy of Achievement.

13 Vise and Malseed, 23.

14 Ken Auletta, *Googled: The End of the World as We Know It* (New York: Penguin Press, 2009), 33.

14 Vise and Malseed, 25.

14 Page, "Larry Page's Commencement Address."

14 American Academy of Achievement.

14 Verne Kopytoff, "Larry Page's Connections: A Conversation with Chronicle Staff Writer Verne Kopytoff," SFGate.com, December 31, 2000, http://www.sfgate.com/cgi-bin/article.cgi?f=/c/a/2000/21/31/BU178263.DTL (June 29, 2009).

15 Page, "Larry Page's Commencement Address."

15 John Battelle, *The Search: How Google and Its Rivals Rewrote the Rules of Business and Transformed Our Culture* (New York: Portfolio, 2005), 66.

15 Ibid., 68.

17 Mark Malseed, "The Story of Sergey Brin: How the Moscow-Born Entrepreneur Cofounded Google and Changed the Way the World Searches," *Moment*, February 2007, http://www.momentmag.com/Exclusive/2007/2007-02/200702-BrinFeature.html (April 4, 2009).

19 Ibid.

20 American Academy of Achievement.

21 Stephanie Strom, "Billionaire Aids Charity That Aided Him," *New York Times*, October 24, 2009, http://www.nytimes.com/2009/10/25/us/25donate.html?_r=1 (November 5, 2009).

21 Janet Lowe, *Google Speaks: Secrets of the World's Greatest Billionaire Entrepreneurs, Sergey Brin and Larry Page* (Hoboken, NJ: John Wiley & Sons, 2009), 16.

22 Battelle, 68.

23 Vise and Malseed, 33.

24 Page, "Larry Page's Commencement Address."

26 Tim Berners-Lee and Mark Fischetti, *How the Web Was Born: The Story of the World Wide Web* (New York: HarperBusiness, 2000), 4.

27 Page, "Larry Page's Commencement Address."

27 Battelle, 73.

27 Page, "Larry Page's Commencement Address."

28 Ibid.

30 Vise and Malseed, 34.

30 Ibid.

31 Battelle, 74.

31 Ibid., 76.

33 Vise and Malseed, 39.

33 Ibid.

33 Ibid.

35 Vise and Malseed, 40.

35   Page, "Larry Page's Commencement Address."

35   Virginia Scott, *Google* (Westport, CT: Greenwood Press, 2008), 32.

36   Page, "Larry Page's Commencement Address."

37   Vise and Malseed, 43.

37   Ibid.

37   Auletta, 40.

38   Vise and Malseed, 48.

38   Battelle, 85.

40   Auletta, 45.

40   Scott, 33.

40   Vise and Malseed, 50.

40   Ibid., 51.

43   Ibid., 68.

43   Ibid.

46   Ibid., 75.

47   Nicholas Carr, *The Big Switch: Rewiring the World, from Edison to Google* (New York: W. W. Norton & Company, 2009), 67.

49   Vice and Malseed, 196, 199.

49   Ibid., 98.

51   Battelle, 124.

51   Auletta, 91.

52   Dennis Hwang, "Oodles of Doodles," Official Google Blog, July 8, 2004, http://googleblog.blogspot.com/2004/06/oodles-of-doodles.html (August 15, 2009).

53   Battelle, 125.

53   Ibid., 135.

54   Ibid.

55   Randall A. Stross, *Planet Google: One Company's Audacious Plan to Organize Everything We Know* (New York: Free Press, 2008), 89.

55   Vise and Malseed, 110.

55   Battelle, 138.

56   Vise and Malseed, 101.

56   Lowe, 90.

59   Auletta, 114.

61   Richard A. Wiggins, "The Effects of September 11 on the Leading Search Engine," *First Monday* 7, no. 10 (October 2001), 2009, http://firstmonday.org/issues/issues6_10/wiggins/index/html (October 1, 2009).

62   Google, "Google Corporate Information: Google Milestones," 2009, http://www.google.com/corporate/history.html (July 12, 2009).

62   Vise and Malseed, 11.

62   Ibid.

62   Ibid., 14.

62   Google, "Google Gets Message, Launches Gmail," April 1, 2004, http://www.google.com/press/pressrel/gmail.html (June 11, 2010).

63   Stross, 90.

66   David Sheff, "Playboy Interview: Google Guys," *Playboy*, September 2004, http://www.google-watch.org/playboy.html (April 17, 2009).

67   Scott, 67.

67   Ibid.

67   Ibid.

67   Auletta, 286.

69   Reuters, Lisa Baertlein, "Google: 'Gmail' No Joke, But Lunar Jobs Are," *USA TODAY*, April 1, 2004, http://www.usatoday.com/tech/news/2004-04-01-gmail-no-joke_x.htm (November 1, 2009).

69   Ibid.

69   Vise and Malseed, 159.

71   Page and Brin, "2004 Founders' IPO Letter."

72   Battelle, 219.

72–73   Sheff.

73   Ibid.

73   Ibid.

74   Battelle, 227.

75   Associated Press, Bradley S. Klapper, "Aid Groups Enlist Google to Help in Haiti Effort," PhysOrg.com, March 2, 2010, http://www.physorg.com/news186760162.html (June 12, 2010).

76   Auletta, 59.

77–78   Stross, 125.

77   Brandt, 168.

77   Mike Swift, "Google's Book Project May Change Copyright Law," MercuryNews.com, March 10, 2010, http://www.mercurynews.com/books/ci_14647600?nclick_=1 (March 10, 2010).

81   Vise and Malseed, 268.

82   David Sarno and Jessica Guynn, "Google Says It's in Talks with China," *Los Angeles Times*, March 10, 2010, http://www.latimes.com/business/la-fi-china-google11-2010mar11,0,7804758,print.story (March 11, 2010).

82 Jessica E. Vascellaro and Loretta Chao, "Google Defies China on Web: Search Giant Stops Censoring Its Results; A Toehold Is in Place in Hong Kong," *Wall Street Journal*, March 23, 2010, 1.

82 Jessica E. Vascellaro, "Brin Led Google to Quit China," *Wall Street Journal*, March 25, 2010, 18.

83 Jia Lynn Yang and Nina Easton, "Obama & Google (a Love Story)," *Fortune* 160, no, 9 (November 9, 2009): 104.

83 Page and Brin, "2004 Founders' IPO Letter."

84 Lowe, 232.

85 Brandt, 222.

90 Verne Kopytoff, Zachary Coile, and Carolyne Zinko, "Now the Other Google Founder Is Planning a Secret Wedding," *San Francisco Chronicle*, November 13, 2007, http://www.sfgate.com/cgi-bin/article.cgi?f=c/a/2007/11/13/BUV6TB3HH.DTL (October 12, 2009).

90 ABC, "For Google Bachelor, a Wedding Fit for a Billionaire," ABC News, December 7, 2007, http://abcnews.go.com/Business/story?id=3969679&page=1 (November 1, 2009).

90 Guy Rolnik, "I've Been Very Lucky in My Life," Haaretz.com, May 29, 2008, http://www.haaretz.co.il/hasen/spages/986222.html (May 7, 2009).

91 Adam Tanner, "Google Founders Have Grown Up, CEO Says," Reuters, May 8, 2008, http://www.reuters.com/article/idUKN0841778920080512 (October 1, 2009).

91 SpaceRef Interactive, "Space Adventures Announces Google Co-Founder Sergey Brin as Orbital Spaceflight Investor and Founding Member of Orbital Mission Explorers Circle," press release, June 11, 2008, Space Adventures, 2009, http://www.spaceref.com/news/viewpr.html?pid=25629 (June 11, 2010).

93 Sergey Brin, "KRRK2," September 18, 2008, http://too.blogspot.com (October 30, 2009).

94 Andrew Pollack, "Google Co-Founder Backs Vast Parkinson's Study," *New York Times*, March 12, 2009, http://www.nytimes.com/2009/03/12/business/12gene.html (October 1, 2009).

95 Jeff Israely, "Italy's Google Verdict Launches Debate on Internet Freedom," *Time*, February 25, 2010, http://www.time.com/time/printout/0,8816,1968123,00.html (February 26, 2010).

95 Ibid.

95 Google, "Google Corporate Information: Google Milestones."

97   Lowe, 240.

97   Stross, 87.

97   Greg Jarboe, "A 'Fireside Chat' with Google's Sergey Brin," Search
     Engine Watch, October 16, 2003, http://searchenginewatch
     .com/3081081 (September 29, 2009).

99   Andy Serwer, "Larry Page on How to Change the World,"
     CNNMoney.com, May 1, 2008, http://money.cnn.com/2008/04/29/
     magazines/fortune/larry_page_change_the_world.fortune/ (October
     2, 2009).

SELECTED BIBLIOGRAPHY

American Academy of Achievement. "Larry Page Interview." Academy of
     Achievement. October 28, 2000. http://www.achievement.org/autodoc/
     page/pag0int-1 (May 4, 2009).

Associated Press and Bloomberg News. "Google Limits China Searches."
     Seattle Times, January 6, 2006. http://seattletimes.nwsource.com/html/
     nationworld/2002762505_chinagoogle26.html (October 1, 2009).

Auletta, Ken. *Googled: The End of the World as We Know It*. New York:
     Penguin Press, 2009.

Battelle, John. *The Search: How Google and Its Rivals Rewrote the Rules of
     Business and Transformed Our Culture*. New York: Portfolio, 2005.

Brandt, Richard L. *Inside Larry and Sergey's Brain*. New York: Portfolio, 2009.

Brin, Sergey. "A Library to Last Forever." *New York Times*, October 9, 2009.
     http://www.nytimes.com/2009/10/09/opinion/09brin.html (October 10,
     2009).

Carr, Nicholas. *The Big Switch: Rewiring the World, from Edison to Google*.
     New York: W. W. Norton & Company, 2009.

Girard, Bernard. *The Google Way: How One Company Is Revolutionizing
     Management as We Know It*. San Francisco: No Starch Press, 2009.

Google. "Corporate Information: Google Milestones." 2009. http://www
     .google.com/corporate/history/html (August 12, 2009).

Gorilovskaya, Nonna. "Online Exclusive—Mark Malseed." *Moment*, April
     2007. http://www.momentmag.com/Exclusive/2007/200/-04/
     200704-GoogleExclusive.html (April 14, 2009).

Hamilton, Joan C. "The Art of the Doodle." *Stanford Magazine*, March–April 2007. http://www.stanfordalumni.org/news/magazine/2007/marapr/features/googledoodler.html (July 9, 2009).

Jarboe, Greg. "A 'Fireside Chat' with Google's Sergey Brin." Search Engine Watch. October 16, 2003. http://searchenginewatch.com/3081081 (September 1, 2009).

Kedar, Ruth. "Ruth Kedar on Designing the Google Logo." Google Blogoscoped. January 14, 2008. http://blogoscoped.com/archive/2008-01-14-n16,html (August 10, 2009).

Lowe, Janet. *Google Speaks: Secrets of the World's Greatest Billionaire Entrepreneurs, Sergey Brin and Larry Page.* Hoboken, NJ: John Wiley & Sons, 2009.

Malseed, Mark. "The Story of Sergey Brin: How the Moscow-Born Entrepreneur Cofounded Google and Changed the Way the World Searches." *Moment*, February 2007. http://www.momentmag.com/Exclusive/2007/2007-02/200702-BrinFeature.html (September 4, 2009).

New York Times. "Google Goes Public." August 20, 2004. http://www.nytimes.com/2004/08/20/opinion/20fri1.html?pagewanted=print (August 22, 2009).

Page, Larry. "Larry Page's University of Michigan Commencement Address." Google Press Center. May 2, 2009. http://www.google.com/intl/en/press/annc/20090502-page-commencement.html (May 6, 2009).

Page, Larry, and Sergey Brin. "2004 Founders' IPO Letter, from the S-1 Registration Statement: 'An Owner's Manual' for Google's Shareholders." Google. 2009. http://investor.google.com/corporate/2004/ipo-founders-letter.html (September 26, 2009).

Pollack, Andrew. "Google Co-Founder Backs Vast Parkinson's Study." *New York Times*, March 12, 2009. http://www.nytimes.com/2009/03/12/business/12gene.html (October 1, 2009).

Reuters, Baertlein, Lisa. "Google: 'Gmail' No Joke, but Lunar Jobs Are." *USA TODAY*, April 1, 2004. http://www.usatoday.com/tech/news/2004-04-01-gmail-no-joke_x.htm (September 26, 2009).

Rolnik, Guy. "I've Been Very Lucky in My Life." Haaretz.com. May 29, 2008. http://www.haaretz.co.il/hasen/spages/986222.html (May 7, 2009).

Sheff, David. "Playboy Interview: Google Guys." *Playboy*, September 2004. http://www.google-watch.org/playboy.html (April 17, 2009).

Stross, Randall. "For the 2008 Race, Google Is a Crucial Constituency." *New York Times*, December 2, 2007. http://www.nytimes.com/2007/12/02/business/02digi.html (September 3, 2009).

———. *Planet Google: One Company's Audacious Plan to Organize Everything We Know*. New York: Free Press, 2008.

Tanner, Adam. "Google Founders Have Grown Up, CEO Says." Reuters. May 8, 2008. http://www.reuters.com/article/idUKN0841778920080512 (October 1, 2009).

Vise, David A., and Mark Malseed. *The Google Story*. Updated edition. New York: Delta Trade Paperbacks, 2008.

Von Bechtolsheim, Andreas. "Von Bechtolsheim: I Invested in Google to Solve My Own Problem." Interview, *Deutsche Welle*. August 12, 2009. http://www.dw-world.de/popups/popup_printcontent/0,,4557608,00.html (August 17, 2009).

Wiggins, Richard A. "The Effects of September 11 on the Leading Search Engine." *First Monday* 7, no. 10 (October 2001). 2009. http://firstmonday.org/issues/issues6_10/wiggins/index.html (September 3, 2009).

FURTHER READING AND WEBSITES

Books
Firestone, Mary. *Wireless Technology*. Minneapolis: Lerner Publications Company, 2009.

Lesinski, Jeanne M. *Bill Gates*. Minneapolis: Twenty-First Century Books, 2009.

McPherson, Stephanie Sammartino. *Tim Berners-Lee: Inventor of the World Wide Web*. Minneapolis: Twenty-First Century Books, 2009.

Sherman, Josepha. *The History of the Internet*. New York: Franklin Watts, 2003.

Stewart, Gail. *Larry Page and Sergey Brin: The Google Guys*. San Diego: KidHaven Press, 2008.

White, Casey. *Sergey Brin and Larry Page: The Founders of Google*. New York: Rosen Publishing Group, 2007.

Websites
American Academy of Achievement—Larry Page Interview
http://www.achievement.org/autodoc/page/pag0int-1
This question-and-answer session with Larry Page gives biographical information on the founders of Google, including memories from Page's childhood and the founding of the company.

Google Corporate Information—Google Milestones
http://www.google.com/corporate/history.html
This website presents a timeline of Google's history from 1995 through the present.

Holiday Logos and Events—Google Style
http://www.google.com/logos/
Enjoy the Google doodles presented around the world from the first Burning Man doodle in 1999 through the present.

The Story of Sergey Brin
http://www.momentmag.com/Exclusive/2007/2007-02/200702-BrinFeature.html
Author Mark Malseed talks with Michael and Eugenia Brin about Sergey's childhood.

PHOTO ACKNOWLEDGMENTS

ABOUT THE AUTHOR

Stephanie Sammartino McPherson wrote her first children's story in college.
She enjoyed the process so much that she's never stopped writing. A former
teacher and freelance newspaper writer, she has written twenty-eight books
and numerous magazine stories. She especially enjoys writing about science
and the human interest stories behind major discoveries. Her most recent
book is a biography of *Tim Berners-Lee*, who invented the World Wide Web.
Stephanie and her husband, Richard, live in Virginia but also call California
home. They are the parents of two grown children.